500 PLASTIC JEWELRY DESIGNS

500 PLASTIC JEWELRY DESIGNS

A GROUNDBREAKING SURVEY OF A MODERN MATERIAL

LARK BOOKS

A Division of Sterling Publishing Co., Inc.
New York / London

SENIOR EDITOR
Marthe Le Van

EDITOR
Julie Hale

ART DIRECTOR
Matt Shay

COVER DESIGNER
Matt Shay

FRONT COVER
Anastasia Azure *Egg Hunt,* 2007

BACK COVER, CLOCKWISE FROM TOP LEFT
Jocelyn Kolb *Maelstrom,* 2007

Edward Lane McCartney *Vaseline Necklace,* 2006

Moshiko Botser *Io (Bracelet),* 2007

Rebecca Strzelec
Cross Section 9, from Army-Green Orchids, 2006

SPINE
Adam Paxon *Bangle,* 2005

FRONT FLAP, FROM TOP
Burcu Büyükünal *Burcu Brooch,* 2005

Geoff Riggle
Vessel of Grace, Faith, and Empty Space, 2007

BACK FLAP
Seainin Passi *Resin Droplet Neckpiece,* 2007

TITLE PAGE
Jocelyn Kolb *Heliotroph,* 2008

OPPOSITE
Seainin Passi *Hot-Melt Glue Ring,* 2007

Library of Congress Cataloging-in-Publication Data

500 plastic jewelry designs: a groundbreaking survey of a modern
material / senior editor, Marthe Le Van. -- 1st ed.
   p. cm.
 Includes index.
 ISBN 978-1-60059-340-6 (pb-pbk. with deluxe flaps : alk. paper)
 1. Plastic jewelry--Catalogs. I. Le Van, Marthe. II. Title: Five hundred
plastic jewelry designs.
 NK4890.P55A24 2009
 745.594'2--dc22

                                           2009000745

10 9 8 7 6 5 4 3 2 1

First Edition

Published by Lark Books, A Division of
Sterling Publishing Co., Inc.
387 Park Avenue South, New York, NY 10016

Text © 2009, Lark Books, a Division of Sterling Publishing Co., Inc.
Photography © 2009, Artist/Photographer

Distributed in Canada by Sterling Publishing,
c/o Canadian Manda Group, 165 Dufferin Street
Toronto, Ontario, Canada M6K 3H6

Distributed in the United Kingdom by GMC Distribution Services,
Castle Place, 166 High Street, Lewes, East Sussex, England BN7 1XU

Distributed in Australia by Capricorn Link (Australia) Pty Ltd.,
P.O. Box 704, Windsor, NSW 2756 Australia

If you have questions or comments about this book, please contact:
Lark Books
67 Broadway
Asheville, NC 28801
828-253-0467

Manufactured in China

ISBN 13: 978-1-60059-340-6

For information about custom editions, special sales, premium and cor-
porate purchases, please contact Sterling Special Sales Department at
800-805-5489 or specialsales@sterlingpub.com.

Contents

Introduction

Throughout history man has taken creative license in finding and using the raw materials of his environment. Early civilizations employed seashells for barter and adornment and relied on pigments from plants and insects to color textiles and paint on walls. Eggs have long served as a base for tempera. Fast-forward to the twentieth century, and we find artists like Damian Hirst, who uses formaldehyde in his work; Fred Tomaselli, who embeds pharmaceuticals in resin on his canvases, and Gordon Matta-Clark, who bisected architectural ruins and made negative space an integral part of his design aesthetic.

The art of jewelry making is no exception to the phenomenon of appropriation, as this book proves. Dedicated to plastics—manufactured products typically used for purposes other than the crafting of jewelry—this volume features a remarkable variety of work employing materials such as resin, latex, rubber, epoxy, and thermoplastics. Having been embraced by artists and designers, these materials are now firmly woven into the language of contemporary jewelry making. Used alone or in combination with traditional elements, these substances can, with certainty, be classified as precious. Thanks to the use of plastics, conventional components like silver, gold, platinum, and gemstones are now only part of the jewelry-making equation.

One of the first plastics to become fashionable with jewelry makers was Bakelite. Invented in 1907, it was the first totally synthetic plastic. Around the time of World War II, a major surge in plastics research occurred in the United States and Europe. During this period, synthetics were developed to replace materials—including metals—that were becoming scarce. Over the decades, countless types of plastics have been developed—including acrylic, vinyl, and epoxy—and the material's reputation as a viable jewelry-making component has grown.

An early champion of plastics as creative media was Harry Hollander, a chemist with the heart of an artist. Hollander worked as an industrial research and development chemist from the 1950s through the 1970s. He spent time at the Penland School of Crafts and the Haystack Mountain School of Crafts, where he was encouraged to pursue his interest in art using his knowledge of resins and plastics. Hollander, with his chemistry skills and laboratory paraphernalia,

Jantje Fleischhut
Neighborhood Series: w.401 | 2005

Lisa Cylinder
Scott Cylinder
Fantasia Piper Brooch/Object | 2005

deciphered the necessary formulas and made resin feasible for use by artists.

Thanks to the books Hollander wrote and the teaching he did in Australia and the United States, he was instrumental in making the arts community aware of plastics. Now resin is available in just about any hardware shop, and most art supply establishments carry pigments that can be used to color resin. Sheet plastics are sold at a host of retail stores.

The jewelry in this collection represents the best work being produced today by artists who use plastics as a foundational element in their pieces. A host of forms and styles is featured on these pages. Narrative pieces, work that expresses environmental concerns, and jewelry that makes clever use of everyday items like paper clips and rubber bands are included. These are pieces that span the realms of the sublime and the humorous. Whether meant for everyday adornment or making a specific statement, for telling a story or giving straightforward aesthetic pleasure, these creations demonstrate the range of possibilities that plastic affords.

We can't help but smile at Margherita De Martino Norante's . . . *Che Fortuna!*—a group of neon-yellow rings that resemble little people—and at Aud Charlotte Ho Sook Sinding's *Parrot*, perched upon a model's shoulder. Through the juxtaposition of mixed materials, a special elegance is achieved in Jantje Fleischhut's *Sateliten 2 Series*, Adam Paxon's highly reflective *Squirming Rings with Tails*, and Pavel Herynek's black-and-white *Winter Landscape* brooches. There is great intricacy in Peter Chang's untitled bracelet and Suzanne Golden's colorful *Bauble-Licious* neckpiece. And we smile again at the charm and cleverness in pieces that incorporate found objects, including Lisa and Scott Cylinder's *Fantasia Piper Brooch/Object*, Margaux Lange's *Silver Shoes Bracelet*, and Rebecca Strzelec's *Mourning Bracelet 2*.

Selecting the extraordinary jewelry you see here was a wonderful experience. The diversity of the work on these pages is proof of the rich potential plastics possess as a medium. I hope that the skill of the designers represented in this book will serve as an inspiration for other artists. I feel privileged to present their work to you.

–Susan Kasson Sloan, Juror

Courtney Starrett
Domestic Goddess | 2008
15 X 11 X 15 CM
Silicone rubber, grommets; slip cast, solid cast
PHOTO BY CHRISTINE SZEREDY

Maria Brossa
Untitled | 2008
16 CM IN DIAMETER
Sterling silver, latex;
hand fabricated
PHOTO BY FEDERICO CAVICCHIOLI

Rebecca Hannon

Beatriz Earrings | 2008

4 X 4 X 0.5 CM

Silver, horsehair,
plastics; riveted

PHOTO BY ARTIST

Pavel Herynek
Homage to My Mother (Ring) | 2003
8.5 X 8.9 X 8.4 CM
Plastic; hand fabricated
PHOTO BY MARKÉTA ONDRUŠKOVÁ

Geoff Riggle

Vessel of Grace, Faith, and Empty Space | 2007

CLOSED, 23 X 15 X 15 CM;
OPEN, 45 X 20 X 15 CM

Polyester, nickel silver, sterling silver; laser etched, fabricated

PHOTOS BY JEFFREY SABO

Jantje Fleischhut

Defrost Series: Black and Matterhorn | 2006

5.5 X 7.5 X 4.5 CM

Polystyrene, postcard, thermoplastic, silver,
yellow gem, found plastic

PHOTOS BY ARTIST

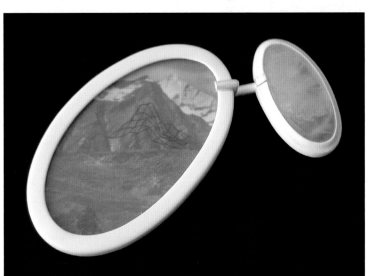

Mary Hallam Pearse
Bling Brooch #7 | 2008
6 X 3.5 X 1.5 CM
Plastic, sterling silver, 14-karat gold, diamonds; cast, fabricated
PHOTO BY ARTIST

Uli

Diamonds and Pearls | 2006

34 X 20 X 0.5 CM

Silicone rubber, textile;
screen-printed

PHOTO BY ARTIST

Pirada Senivongse Na Ayudhya
Untitled | 2006
28 CM LONG
Acrylic, silver; hand dyed, laser cut, hand woven
PHOTO BY VISIONARY

Berenice Ramírez
Untitled Vinyl Neckpiece 2 | 2007
55.9 X 35.6 X 10.2 CM
Vinyl, nylon thread; sewn
PHOTOS BY ARTIST

**Aud Charlotte Ho
Sook Sinding**
Anita | 2006
40 X 22 X 8 CM
Silicone, silver, textile;
hollow cast
PHOTO BY ARTIST

Influenced by historic lace collars,
Flesh Collar #1 acts as a patterned
skin that mimics bodily transformation. JBG

Jill K. Baker Gower
Flesh Collar #1 | 2006
18.5 X 18.5 X 0.4 CM
Silicone rubber, sterling silver, cubic
zirconium, glass buttons; chased,
repoussé, poured, stone setting
PHOTO BY ARTIST

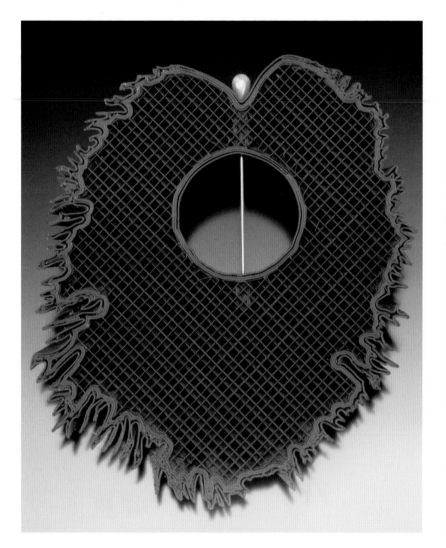

Rebecca Strzelec

*Cross Section 9, from
Army-Green Orchids* | 2006

12 X 10.4 X 1.7 CM

FDM plastic, corsage pin;
rapid prototyped, CAD

PHOTOS BY DOUG YAPLE

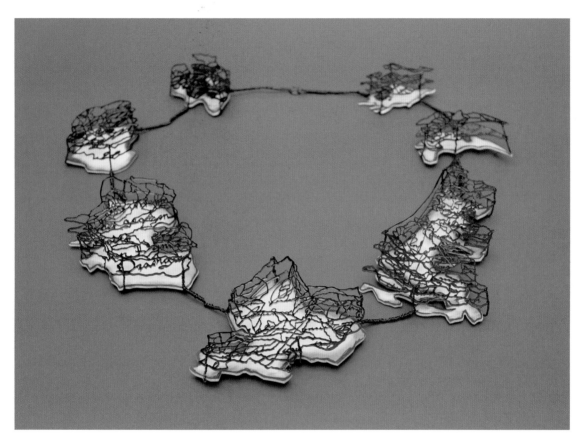

Francis Willemstijn
Necklace for Willem van Oranje | 2007
40 CM IN LENGTH
Polystyrene, iron
PHOTO BY ARTIST

Ellen Himic
Swirl Brooch | 2006
12.1 X 12.1 X 5.1 CM
Epoxy resin; rapid prototyped
PHOTO BY SELECTIVE PHOTOGRAPHY

**Nervous System
(Jessica Rosenkrantz and
Jesse Louis-Rosenberg)**
Orchid Necklace | 2008
2.3 X 8.4 X 8.6 CM
Polystyrene, silk; laser cut
PHOTO BY ARTISTS

Christiane Schorm

Rainbow Chain | 2008

0.8 X 4.4 X 54 CM

Sterling silver, photopolymers;
hand fabricated

PHOTO BY ELMAR WOLFF

Nari Lee

Hana | 2008

11 X 1.5 X 1.5 CM

Acrylic sheets, sterling
silver; polished

PHOTO BY MYUNG WOOK HUH

Ana Margarida Carvalho

A Door Without a Knob is a Wall | 2007

VARIOUS DIMENSIONS

Nylon, silver; spun, dyed, soldered

PHOTO BY ARTIST

I feel the power and delicacy of the materials is expressed in both light and shade. The light that passes through colorful resin is beautiful and poetic. MI

Meiri Ishida
Spiral City (Bracelet) | 2006
5 X 13 X 13 CM
Acrylic resin, felt, polycarbonate, glass, silver; hand fabricated
PHOTO BY ARTIST

27

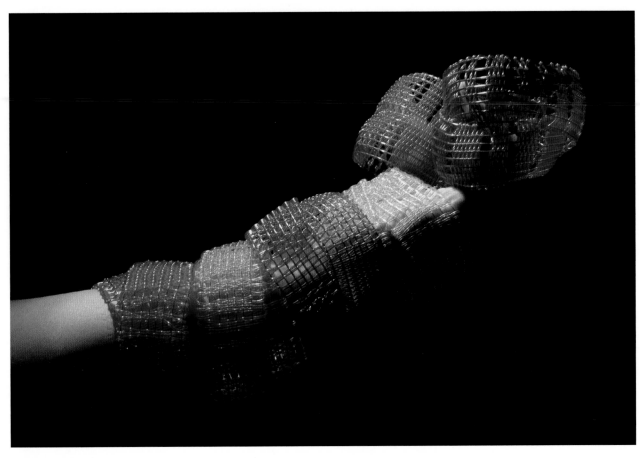

Hsueh-Ying Wu

Infinite I | 2006

EACH, 8 X 6 CM

Plastic tube, stainless steel
string; hand fabricated

PHOTO BY CHIN-TING CHIU

Burcu Büyükünal

Burcu Brooch | 2005

4 X 4 X 1 CM

Plastic drinking straws, thermoplastic,
stainless steel; lathe turned, assembled

PHOTO BY ARTIST

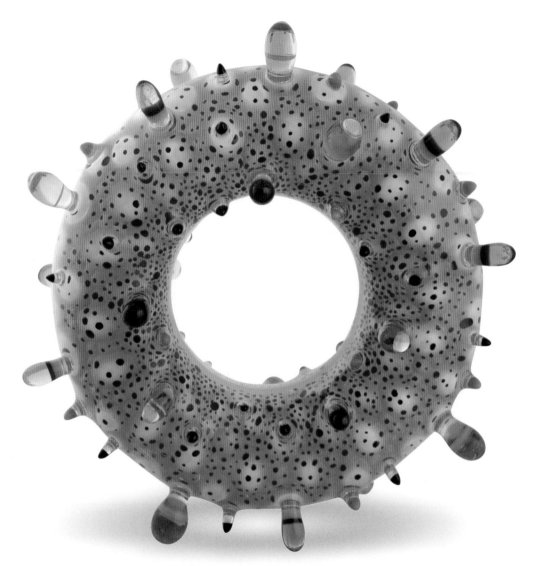

Adam Paxon

Bangle | 2005

16.5 X 16.5 X 8 CM

Acrylic, epoxy; laminated, thermoformed,
hand carved, polished

PHOTO BY PAUL AMBTMAN

Aud Charlotte Ho Sook Sinding
From the Vanitas Series | 2008
28 X 18 X 10 CM
Silicone, polyurethane plastic,
beads; hollow cast, flocked
PHOTO BY ARTIST

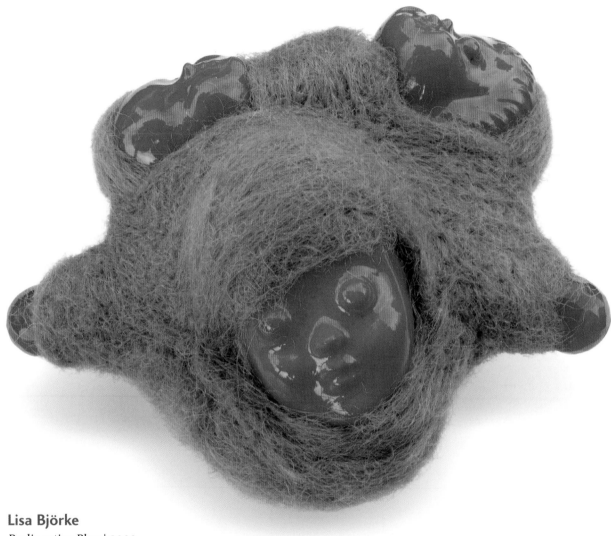

Lisa Björke

Radioactive Play | 2008

6 X 8 X 3.5 CM

Wool, plastic doll faces, spray paint, epoxy resin, iron, dental wire; needle felted

PHOTO BY ARTIST

Felieke van der Leest
Chimp Champ | 2001
MONKEY, 4.5 X 6 X 4.5 CM
Plastic nuts, plastic animal, textile,
silver, gold; crocheted, metalsmithed
PHOTO BY EDDO HARTMANN

Atelier Ted Noten

Fred (Fly with Pearl) | 2004

4 X 2.5 X 1.2 CM

Fly, pearl, acrylic; cast

PHOTO BY ARTIST

Sun Kyoung Kim
Finger 02 | 2006
5.1 X 5.1 X 5.1 CM
Sterling silver, resin; cast
PHOTOS BY ARTIST

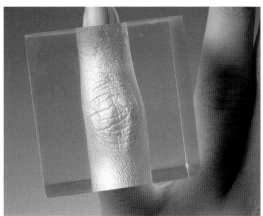

Claudia Gieger
Ling Necklace | 2006
45 CM LONG
Polypropylene, 18-karat gold, stainless
steel wire; stamped, gold plated
PHOTO BY ARTIST

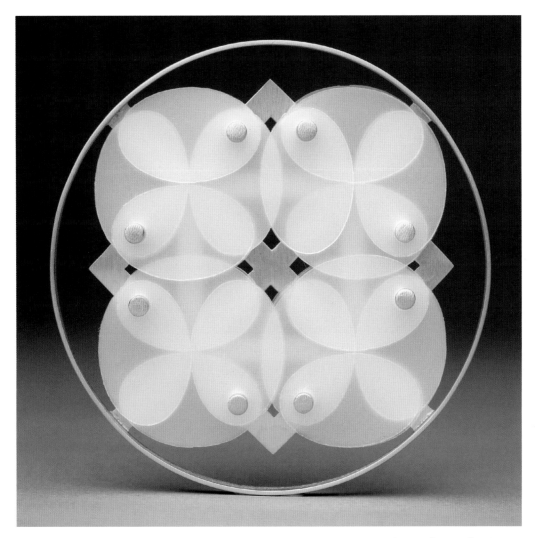

Christel van der Laan
Priceless Brooch | 2006
6.3 X 6.3 X 0.7 CM
Gold-plated sterling silver,
polypropylene price tags
PHOTO BY ROBERT FRITH

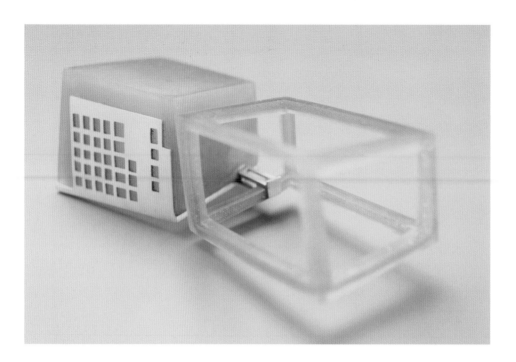

Jantje Fleischhut

Neighborhood Series: b.270 and *w.401* | 2005

LARGEST, 4 X 7 X 10 CM

Epoxy, fiberglass, citrine, 14-karat gold

PHOTOS BY EDDO HARTMANN

Eunyoung Park
Winter Landscape III | 2006
4 X 2.5 X 1 CM
Sterling silver, thermoplastic
PHOTO BY ARTIST

39

Josephine Winther
Fugue | 2003
EACH, 3 X 2 X 0.2 CM
Silver, resin
PHOTO BY DORTE KROGH

Seainin Passi

Resin Droplet Neckpiece | 2007

25 X 30 X 20 CM

Polyester resin, mild steel wire, steel
fuse wire; wrapped, soldered, shaped

PHOTO BY RICHARD BOLL PHOTOGRAPHY

Kyoko Hashimoto

Bubble Rings | 2002

TALLEST, 4 X 2.5 X 2.5 CM

Freshwater pearls, sterling silver, polyester
resin, pigment; cast, hand carved

PHOTO BY ARTIST

Masako Onedera

Voluptuous Appendage | 2006

11.4 X 6.4 X 5.1 CM

Found plastic objects, polyethylene
cord; dyed, crocheted

PHOTO BY ARTIST

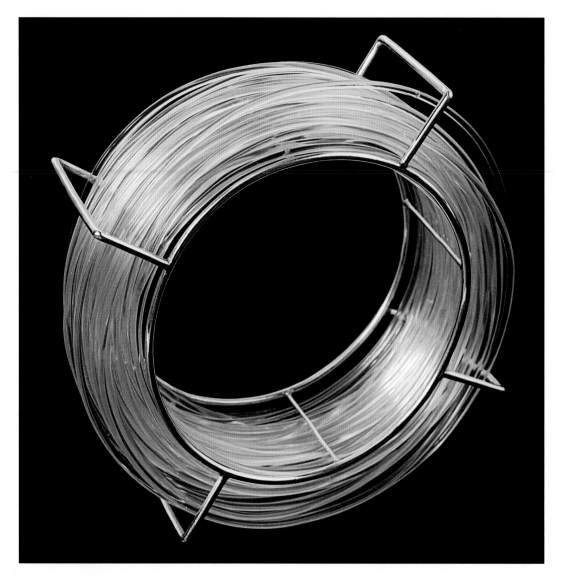

Iro Kaskanis

Untitled | 2002

3.5 X 9.5 X 1.5 CM

Silver, plastic cord;
hand fabricated

PHOTO BY DIMITRIS VATTIS

Shelby Ferris Fitzpatrick
FUSION Neckpiece | 2001
38 X 38 X 5 CM
Thermoplastic, rubber, silver, silk;
constructed, fabricated
PHOTOS BY MIKE BLISSETT

Nora Fok
Armadillo | 2007
30 CM IN DIAMETER
Clear nylon; woven
PHOTOS BY FRANK HILLS

I use the traditional technique of bobbin lace with modern materials like fishing line or metal wire to find new ways of expression. The lace can be formed into three-dimensional objects that are characterized by transparency and preciousness. SK

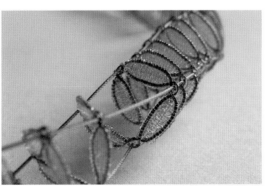

Stefanie Kölbel
450 Leaves | 2006
1 X 16 X 22 CM
High-grade steel wire, fishing line;
bobbin lace, dyed
PHOTOS BY ARTIST

Yuka Saito
Ocean | 2006
50 X 22 X 6 CM
Polypropylene, nylon
PHOTO BY DEAN POWELL

Mona Wallstrom
Double Icebell Brooch | 2006
9 X 4 X 2.5 CM
Acrylic, horsehair,
silver; hand milled
PHOTO BY ARTIST

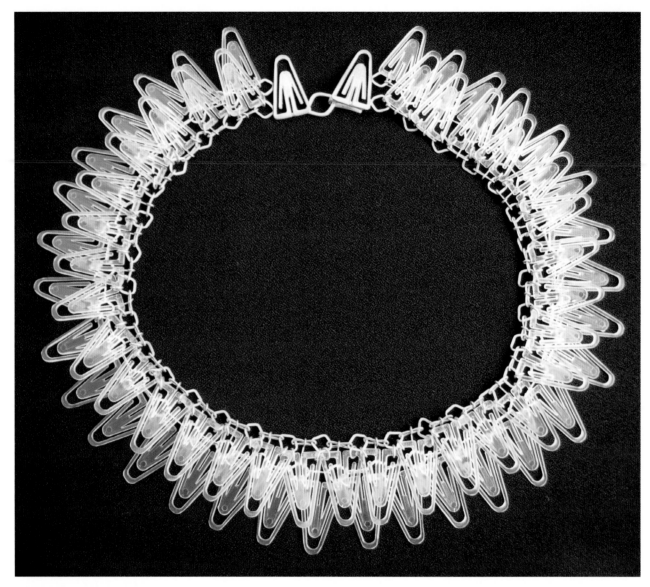

LaVerne Christenson
Paperklip Necklace | 2007
Plastic paperclips,
sterling silver; cast
PHOTO BY ARTIST

Eva Hestbek Jensen
From Bucket to Bouquet | 2008
35 X 22 X 1 CM
Plastic bucket
PHOTO BY DORTE KROGH

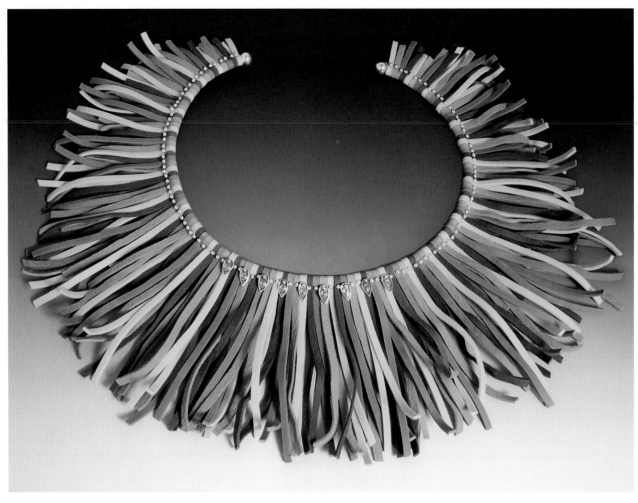

Sosan Keane

Afrikaan Essence | 2008

23 X 26 CM

Rubber bands, sterling silver;
riveted, fabricated

PHOTO BY ARTIST

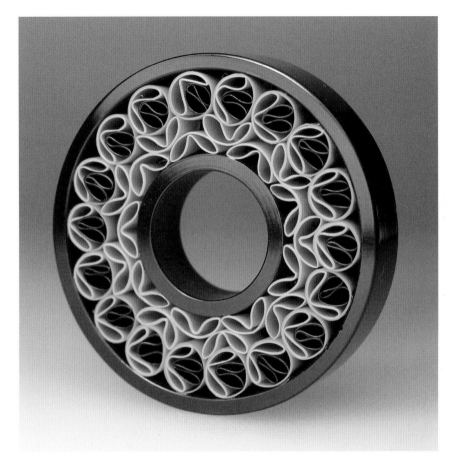

Burcu Büyükünal
Burcu Brooch | 2005
4 X 4 X 1 CM
Plastic drinking straws, thermoplastic, stainless
steel, epoxy; lathe turned, assembled
PHOTO BY ARTIST

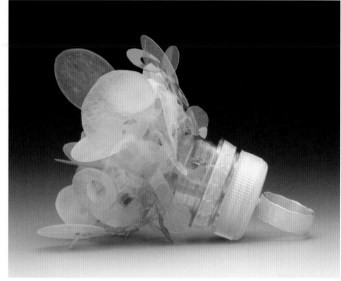

Liaung Chung Yen
Changeability #1 (Pendant/Ring) | 2007
8 X 8 X 8 CM
Plastic bottle and cap, plastic sheet,
sterling silver; cut, fabricated
PHOTOS BY ARTIST

Marie Asbjørnsen
Belonging; Global | 2008
28 X 6 CM
World map, plastic sailcloth,
sterling silver, coated steel wire
PHOTO BY ARTIST

Edward Lane McCartney
Fishing Neckpiece | 2007
8 X 40 X 60 CM
Fishing floats, steel cable,
sterling silver
PHOTO BY ARTIST

Carolyn Tillie
Ama-Ebi Necklace | 2008
1.6 X 6 X 0.5 CM
14-karat gold, plastic
sushi; fabricated
PHOTO BY WWW.RICHARDMATZINGER.COM

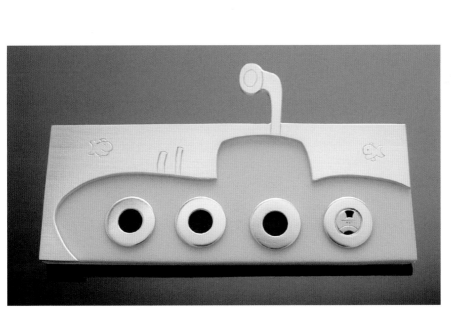

Eero Hintsanen
Yellow Submarine | 2007
3.8 X 6.7 X 0.9 CM
Sterling silver, foam rubber;
hand engraved, fabricated,
gold plated
PHOTO BY CHAO-HSIEN KUO

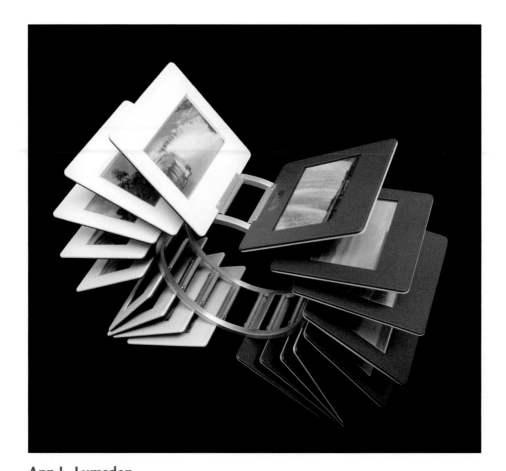

Ann L. Lumsden

Vacation (Bracelet) | 2004

17 X 5 CM

Sterling silver, vintage postcards, plastic
and glass slide mounts, steel spring bars;
hand fabricated, riveted

PHOTO BY ARTIST

Katalin H. Markus
Untitled | 2007
5.8 X 4.8 X 0.8 CM
Acrylic, silver
PHOTO BY JACK B. ZILKER

Maarten van der Vegte
Hong Nan Lü Nü | 2006
3 X 7 X 1.5 CM
Thermoplastic, resin,
sterling silver, steel
PHOTO BY ARTIST

Stephanie Ellis

Adornment Object #1 | 2008

30 X 20 X 1 CM

Plastic earpieces, wire

PHOTO BY ARTIST

Jennifer Theokary

Flex #2 | 2006

12.7 X 12.7 X 10.2 CM

Sterling silver, resin, steel; carved,
cast, fabricated

PHOTO BY ARTIST

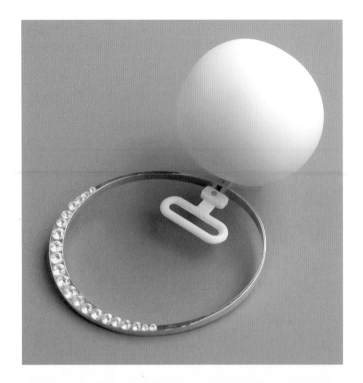

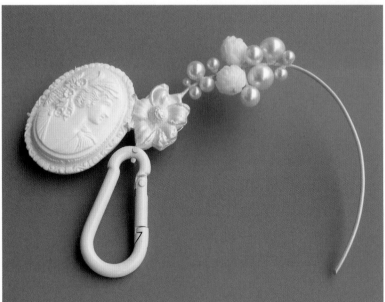

Jantje Fleischhut

Die Weissen Berge Series:
Luminary and Spring-Hook Branch | 2007

TALLEST, 4 X 8.5 X 5 CM

Epoxy, fiberglass, zirconia, silver,
pearls, spring-hook; cast

PHOTOS BY ARTIST

Elizabeth Boyd Hartmann
Hand Pieces | 2006
VARIOUS DIMENSIONS
Resin, fine silver; cast, electroformed
PHOTO BY NICK FALLON

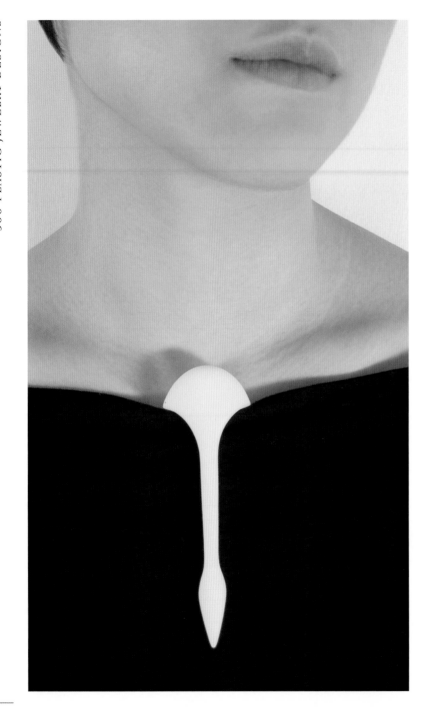

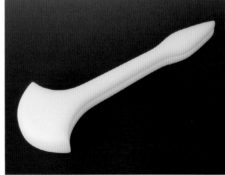

Kevin Hughes
Untitled | 2006
11.4 X 3.8 X 1.9 CM
Resin; carved
PHOTOS BY ARTIST

Svenja John
5T Transformation Bracelet | 2008
11 X 6 CM
Digital material; 3D printed
PHOTO BY JÖRG FAHLENKAMP

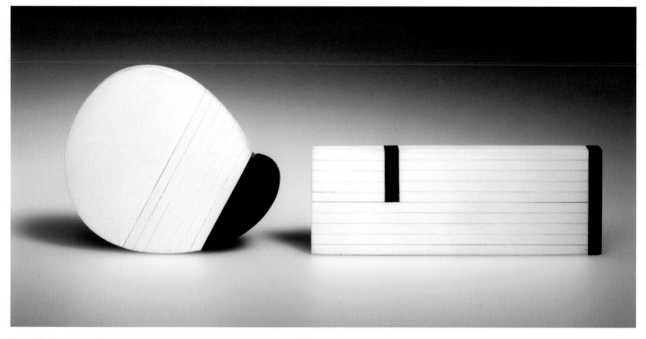

Pavel Herynek
Winter Landscape IV, Winter Landscape I (Brooches) | 2000
LARGEST, 3.1 X 9 X 0.7 CM
Plastic, stainless steel; hand fabricated
PHOTO BY MARKÉTA ONDRUŠKOVÁ

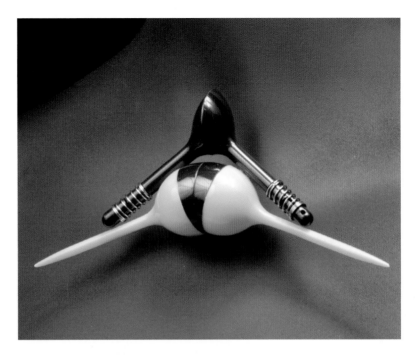

Robly A. Glover
Bobber Fabrication #1 and #2 | 2008
EACH, 6.4 X 16.5 X 3.8 CM
Plastic, steel, earth magnets
PHOTOS BY ARTIST

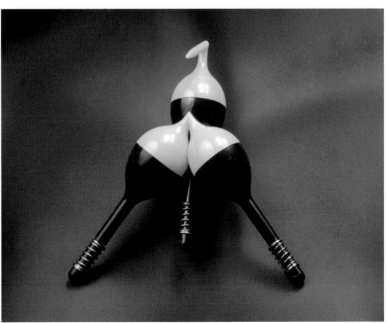

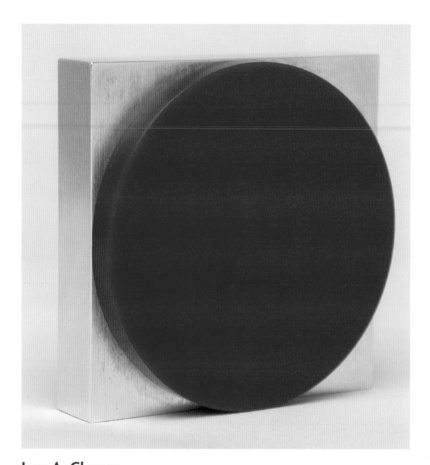

Jens A. Clausen

Red | 2007

5 X 5 X 1.7 CM

Sterling silver, epoxy resin, LED in plastic setting,
stainless steel; fabricated, turned, assembled

PHOTO BY ARTIST

Motoko Furuhashi
Planet Earth (Bracelet) | 2006
6 X 12 X 12 CM
Sterling silver, acrylic;
fabricated, vacuformed
PHOTO BY ARTIST

Carole Leonard
Checked Bangle | 2003
8.4 X 8.4 X 1.9 CM
Thermoplastic, silver;
cut, laminated
PHOTO BY JOHN HYTCH

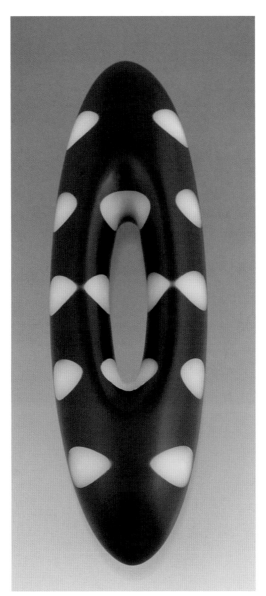

Jon M. Ryan
Untitled | 2008
8.7 X 2.6 X 1 CM
Resin, sterling silver, epoxy;
carved, fabricated
PHOTO BY ARTIST

Gill Forsbrook

Untitled | 2005

10 X 12 X 9 CM

Polypropylene, thermoplastic,
silver; hand fabricated

PHOTO BY ARTIST

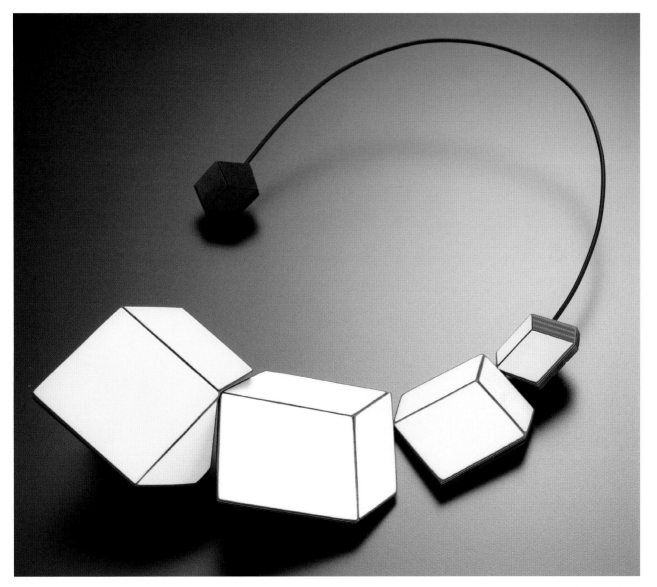

Linda Hughes
Red and White Series: Box Neckpiece | 2008
30 CM IN DIAMETER
Sterling silver, rubber; laminated
PHOTO BY GRANT HANCOCK

Paula Crespo

Black Cylinder (Rings) | 2007

EACH, 3 X 2.2 CM

Vulcanized rubber, gold; turned, fabricated

PHOTO BY JOÁO CARVALHO DE SOUSA

Jin Sun Eo
Turn Round and Round | 2008
EACH, 4.5 X 4.5 X 1.1 CM
Sterling silver, electric wire
PHOTO BY STUDIO MUNCH

Anastasia Azure

Ribbon Candy | 2007

LARGEST, 10 X 10 X 3 CM

Fine silver, sterling silver, copper,
color pigment, nylon monofilament;
dimensional weave, inlaid, fabricated

PHOTO BY HAP SAKWA

Karla Way

Material Worlds (Object to be Suspended) | 2008

11 X 7 X 7 CM

Thermoplastic, sterling silver, copper, enamel, plastic, sand,
epoxy resin adhesive, paint, cubic zirconia, silk cord, cotton;
cold connected

PHOTO BY DOUGAL HASLEM

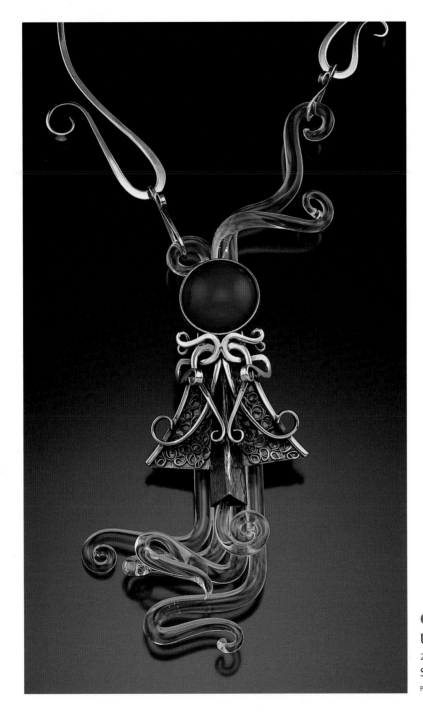

Greg Greenwood
Untitled Neck Adornment | 2006
20 X 6 X 5 CM
Sterling silver, acrylic; fabricated
PHOTO BY LARRY SANDERS

This piece was modeled after the elaborate seventeenth-century lace ruffs worn by court women. It also emulates the stylization of modern chess pieces. JAH

Jung Ah Hahn
Red Queen | 2007
76 X 46 X 18 CM
Polyethylene foam; stitched, heat formed
PHOTO BY THOMAS HILTON

Barbara Cohen
Untitled | 2007
15 X 15 X 3 CM
Nylon mesh, rubber, yarn,
sterling silver; fabricated
PHOTO BY ARTIST

Elva Escobedo-Duran
Mutant 4 | 2007
50 X 7 X 3.5 CM
Thermoplastic, resin, fine
silver, monofilament; dyed
PHOTO BY CHRIST CHAVEZ

Yuh-Shyuan Chen

Actinia Bracelet | 2007

5.7 X 7.8 X 7.3 CM

Aluminum, copper, brass,
rubber toy; fabricated

PHOTO BY ARTIST

Joe Churchman
Hole Bracelet and Noodle Bracelet | 2008
VARIABLE DIMENSIONS
Foam; fabricated
PHOTO BY STEPHEN JOHN ELLIS

Maria Constanza Ochoa
Soft Black and White | 2007
20.1 X 20.2 X 1 CM
Plastic, balloons,
flour; fabricated
PHOTO BY FEDERICO CAVICCHIOLI

Katja Korsawe
Panties | 2008
20 X 15 X 4 CM
Polyamid; twisted
PHOTO BY THOMAS SCHULTZE

Linki van Zyl

Neo-Baroque Neckpiece | 2007

27 X 32 X 1.5 CM

Platinum, discarded acrylic sheet, pigment, resin, garnet beads; hand fabricated, hand painted, laminated

PHOTO BY KEVIN RUDHAM

Kathleen Janvier
Chandelier Pearls | 2007
43 CM LONG; PEARLS, 2 X 2 X 0.8 CM EACH
Sterling silver, resin, ceramic decals;
fabricated, cast, chased, scribed
PHOTOS BY ARTIST

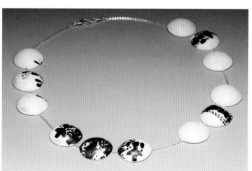

Renée Zettle-Sterling
Object of Mourning #9 (Brooch) | 2007
7 X 11.4 X 4.4 CM
Silver, plastic; fabricated, cast
PHOTO BY DAVID SMITH

Tessa E. Rickard

Little Flora | 2007

6.5 X 3 X 2 CM

Plastic, sterling silver, cubic zirconia,
rubber; cast, glued, fabricated

PHOTO BY TIM CARPENTER

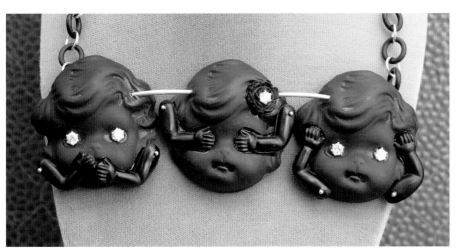

Tessa E. Rickard

Three Golden Rules | 2008

5.1 X 14 X 2.5 CM

Plastic resin, rubber, sterling
silver, cubic zirconia, pigment;
cast, fabricated, formed

PHOTO BY ARTIST

Sun Jin Choi

Eye | 2008

EACH, 0.2 X 6 CM

Film, nickel, silver

PHOTO BY KWANG-CHOON PARK

Sun Kyoung Kim

Palm 01 | 2007

9 X 6.5 X 1.5 CM

Sterling silver, resin; fabricated

PHOTO BY ARTIST

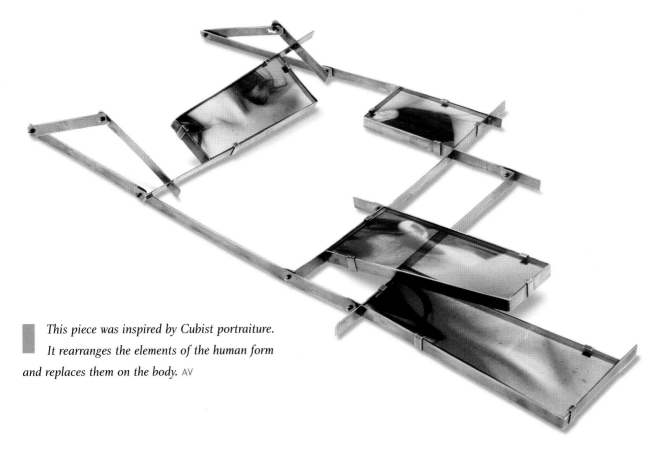

This piece was inspired by Cubist portraiture. It rearranges the elements of the human form and replaces them on the body. AV

Andi Velgos
Self Perception | 2006
36 X 15 X 0.5 CM
Photographic transparencies, acrylic, sterling silver; laminated
PHOTOS BY STEFFEN ALLEN

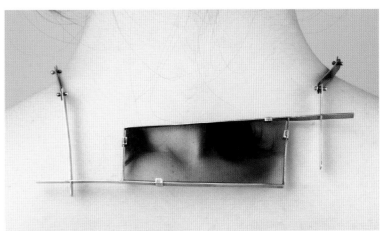

Essor

Dimensions Bracelet | 2006

18 X 4.5 X 1 CM

Sterling silver, transparent
film; hand fabricated

PHOTO BY ARTIST

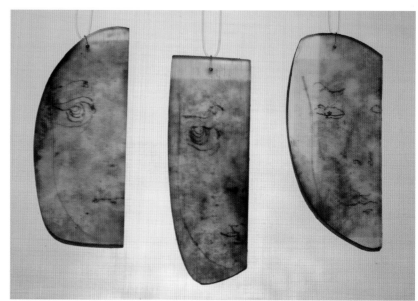

Hoyeon Chung

The Girl | 2008

2.2 X 6 X 0.5 CM

Epoxy resin, oil paper,
acrylic paint; cast

PHOTO BY ARTIST

Gwendolyn McLarty
Headdress | 2008
17 X 12.5 X 5 CM
Paper, polyester film, monofilament;
hand assembled, dyed, laminated
PHOTO BY JACK ZILKER

Sung-Yeoul Lee

Knot So Precious!! | 2007

7.6 X 6.4 X 10.2 CM

Resin, sterling silver, rope;
cast, fabricated

PHOTO BY ARTIST

Teresa Faris
Untitled Brooch | 2007
12.7 X 7.6 X 1.3 CM
Latex, sterling silver,
stainless steel; painted
PHOTO BY ARTIST

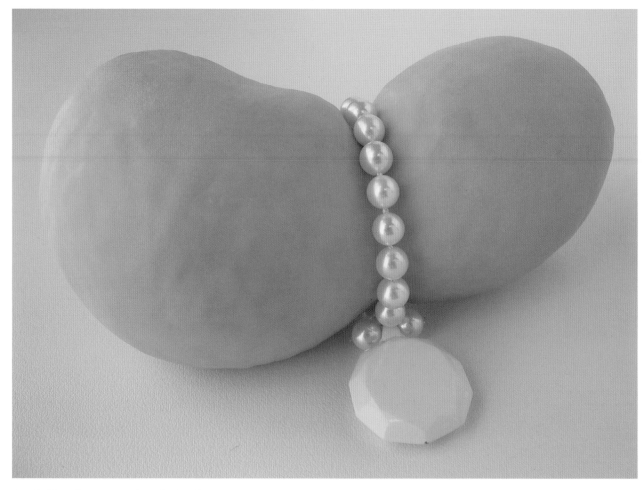

Aud Charlotte Ho Sook Sinding

Christine | 2006

8 X 15 X 6 CM

Silicone, silver, pearls;
hollow cast, lacquered

PHOTO BY ARTIST

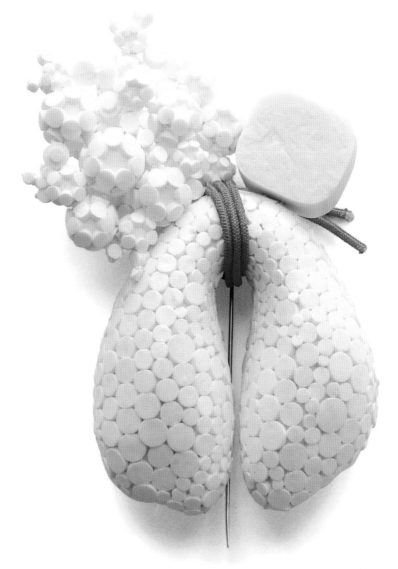

Karin Seufert
Untitled | 2007

9 X 6 X 4 CM

PVC, reconstructed coral, thread,
elastic, steel; sewn, glued, cut

PHOTO BY ARTIST

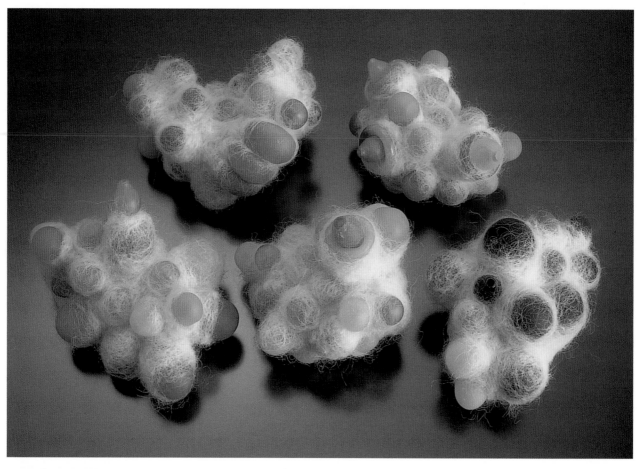

Masako Onedera

Cellular Brooches | 2006

EACH, 8.9 X 7.6 X 5.1 CM

Found plastic objects, wool; dyed, needle felted

PHOTO BY ARTIST

Beate Weiss
Gavalon Open Eyes Ring | 2004
4.5 X 3 CM
Dental plastic,
sterling silver, pearls
PHOTO BY PETRA JASCHKE

The primary material for my rings is dental plastic, a material that was originally developed for use with toothbraces. The material's light weight and sturdiness make it extremely well suited for jewelry making. Dental plastic opened entirely new vistas for me. BW

Rebecca Hannon
Bough Neckpiece | 2008
35 X 22 X 1 CM
Silver, ribbon, plastics; riveted
PHOTO BY ARTIST

Jantje Fleischhut
Echt Plastik | 2004
Epoxy, topaz, rose quartz,
rock crystal; cast
PHOTO BY ARTIST

Sarah Kate Burgess
Cloud, Colander, and Sieve | 2003
VARIOUS DIMENSIONS
Found melamine cups;
cut, sanded, finished
PHOTO BY BILL BACHHUBER

Christiane Schorm
Inside Out | 2008
1.4 X 3 X 62 CM
Sterling silver, photopolymers,
pigments; hand fabricated
PHOTO BY ELMAR WOLFF

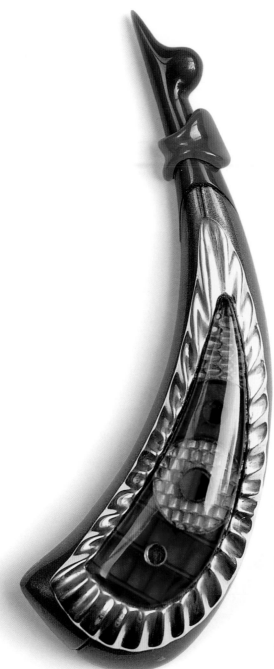

Peter Chang
Untitled Brooch | 2007
11.7 X 3 X 1.3 CM
Acrylic, aluminum, found plastic;
thermoformed, carved, polished
PHOTO BY ARTIST

Josephine Winther
Rubyfruits | 2005
23 X 16 X 3.5 CM
Resin, 18-karat gold,
tassels; cast
PHOTO BY DORTE KROGH

Jennifer Shaline
Gemini | 2006
5.7 X 1.9 X 0.6 CM
Ultraviolet light-sensitive
acrylic; laminated, carved
PHOTO BY LARRY SANDERS

Erina Kashihara
Wearable Illuminant Art:
Light Hulls | 2004
70 X 33 X 34 CM
White LED, epoxy resin,
artificial leather, pulse sensor
mechanism circuit
PHOTO BY KEIICHI TANAKA

Lulu Smith

Red Trapezoid Bracelet | 2004

7 X 1 X 0.3 CM

Sterling silver, resin; hand pigmented

PHOTO BY DOUGLAS YAPLE

Betty Heald

Vessel Brooches | 1999

EACH, 7.5 X 5.5 X 1.5 CM

Acrylic, stainless steel; chemically
dyed, heat formed

PHOTO BY NORMAN WATKINS

Sarah King
Untitled | 2006
2.5 X 49 X 1.5 CM
Bioresin, sterling silver; cast, inlaid
PHOTO BY JEREMY JOHNS PHOTOGRAPHY

Birgit Laken
Spoons Necklace | 2007
38 X 33 X 2.2 CM
Melamine, 14-karat gold
PHOTO BY ARTIST

Katrin Veegen
Soon | 2007
3 X 8 X 5 CM
Jesmonite, cubic zirconia,
silver, wood
PHOTO BY ARTIST

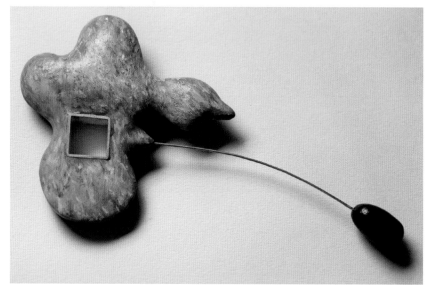

Hu Jun
Untitled | 2008
8.5 X 15.6 X 2.8 CM
Silver, resin, acrylic colors
PHOTO BY ARTIST

Demitra Thomloudis

Directional Black | 2007

6.5 X 3 X 2.5 CM

Sterling silver, cellulose acetate, pearls; carved, fabricated, soldered, chemically fused

PHOTO BY ARTIST

Criaturas are inspired by tantalizing organisms. By inventing these pieces, each with their own unique qualities, functions, and forms, I strive to capture the essence and understand the meaning of creation. CD

Cristina Dias

Criatura # 10 (Bracelet) | 2007

18 X 19 X 10 CM

Silicone rubber, pigments, fibers, wool, steel, beads, magnets; assembled, coated

PHOTO BY ARTIST

Natalya Pinchuk
Growth Series: Brooch | 2007
14 X 7 X 5 CM
Wool, copper, enamel, plastic,
waxed thread, stainless steel;
fabricated, assembled
PHOTO BY ARTIST

Eun Yeong Jeong
New-Born Taro | 2007
9 X 6 X 5.5 CM
Taro, wool, thermoplastics,
stainless steel; hand fabricated
PHOTO BY ARTIST

This piece is part of a series that examines the themes of honor and achievement. Through the series, I was trying to detect the fine line between vanity and earned respect. KV

Katrin Veegen
Heroes of Our Time II (Brooch) | 2006
9 X 4.5 X 2 CM
Jesmonite, silver, cubic zirconia,
wood, cotton, acrylic, paint
PHOTO BY ARTIST

Ela Bauer
Necklace U | 2007
40 X 7 X 4 CM
Silicone, corals, jade, glass
beads; molded, sewn
PHOTO BY ARTIST

Jacomijn van der Donk
Untitled | 2006
110 CM
Beech twig, epoxy, leather, gold
PHOTO BY OLE ESHUIS

Hiltje Wynia
Untitled | 2007
45 X 27 X 3 CM
Acrylic sheet; formed, sprayed
PHOTO BY BIRGIT LAKEN

Kenji Uchino
You Chou Ge | 2007
12 X 11 X 10 CM
Soft resin, feathers,
copper, acrylic colors
PHOTO BY ARTIST

Betty Heald
Untitled (Brooch) | 2008
9 X 9 X 4.5 CM
Epoxy resin, pigments, copper netting,
steel; electroformed, fabricated
PHOTO BY ARTIST

Sayumi Yokouchi

Bloom 1 (Brooch) | 2007

8.5 X 9 X 2.5 CM

Sterling silver, 14-karat white gold,
plastic bottle caps, silk thread

PHOTO BY ARTIST

Nora Fok

The Spirit of Aqualegia (Aquilegia) | 2004

19 CM IN DIAMETER

Pigment, nylon; dyed, woven

PHOTO BY FRANK HILLS

Nisa Blackmon

ZBSS.01805, Brooch with
Type Specimen Reference | 2007

4.5 X 15 X 6 CM

Plastic flowers, plasticized paint, aluminum,
sterling silver; dissected, combined,
tagged, dipped, fabricated, mounted

PHOTO BY ARTIST

The Zoo Botanical Simulated Species (ZBSS) were created
by disassembling and recombining elements of various
plastic flower pieces. The resulting faux-organisms were placed
in jewelry settings to produce wearable specimens. NB

Gitte Nygaard
Opus Formosus Collection:
Flagrare Plexus | 2004–2005
18 X 15 CM
Polyethylene, silver, garnets; cut
PHOTO BY JOSIE SYKES

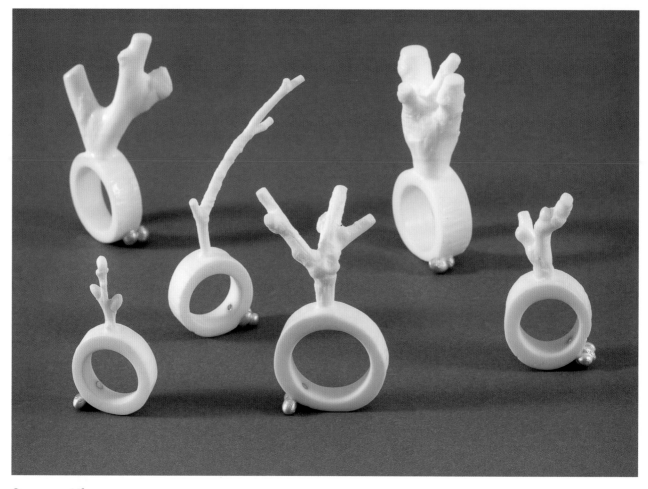

Susanne Klemm

Mutation Rings | 2007

VARIOUS DIMENSIONS

Sterling silver, epoxy
resin; cast

PHOTO BY HAROLD STRAK

Sara Engberg
All Flesh is Grass | 2007
22 X 13 X 0.4 CM
Acrylic, silver
PHOTO BY ARTIST

Susanne Kaube
Überaschung | 2007
EACH, 4.5 CM IN DIAMETER
PVC, gold
PHOTO BY ARTIST

Julia M. Barello
Flowers of Rhetoric: Abcisio | 2007
61 CM IN DIAMETER
Recycled MRI film, monofilament;
laser cut
PHOTO BY MICHAEL O'NEILL

Kath Inglis

Skin-Deep Bangles | 2001

EACH, 3.3 X 7 X 7 CM

PVC, sterling silver; fabricated, hand
colored, hand carved, hand stitched

PHOTO BY MICHAEL HAINES

For just a few minutes, amazing colors appear when oxidizing silver. Lamination freezes the moment. YH

Yael Herman
Black leaves | 2007
2.5 X 2.5 X 200 CM
Silver; oxidized, laminated
PHOTO BY ARTIST

131

Courtney Starrett

Actiniaria | 2008

17.8 X 17.8 X 20.3 CM

Silicone rubber, grommets;
slip cast, solid cast

PHOTO BY CHRISTINE SZEREDY

Velina A. Glass
Fossil | 2008
10.2 X 3.1 X 1.3 CM
Epoxy resin, sterling
silver; cast, fabricated
PHOTO BY JOSEPH HYDE

Svenja John
Hanra Necklace | 2007
50 X 3 CM
Surface-treated polycarbonate;
laser colored, water jet cut
PHOTO BY TIVADAR NEMESI

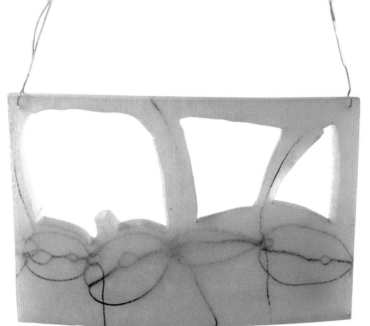

Beate Eismann
Pendant | 2002
11.7 X 17.6 X 1 CM
Artificial resin, wire; cast
PHOTO BY ARTIST

Marianne Schliwinski
Brooch | 2002
4.7 X 6.8 X 0.6 CM
Plastic, tin, glass; mounted
PHOTO BY JÜRGEN EICKHOFF

Heidi Schwegler

Legacy | 2001

183 X 183 X 8 CM

Water-clear urethane, pigment, silicone, sterling silver, steel

PHOTOS BY BILL BACHHUBER

Sung-Yeoul Lee
Ring Series: Knot So Precious | 2007
TALLEST, 4.4 X 3.8 X 2.5 CM
Resin, sterling silver, polypropylene
rope, rope; cast, dipped
PHOTO BY ARTIST

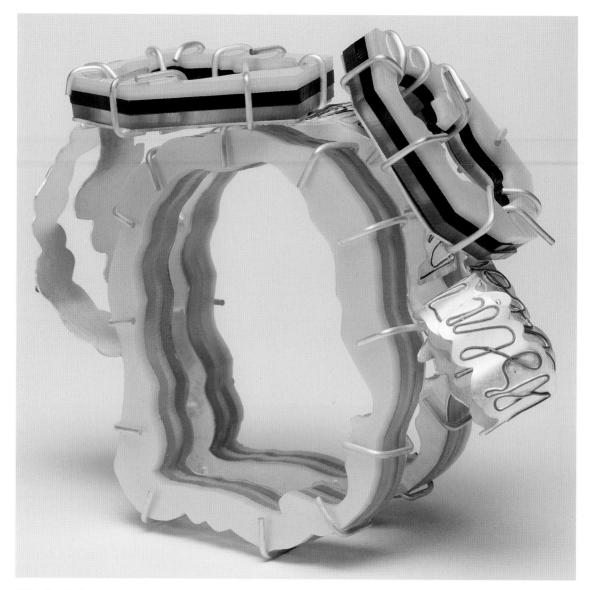

Nicole Polentas

Bracelet Daskalo Gianni | 2007

13.5 X 11 X 6 CM

Sterling silver, copper, thermoplastic; fused, fabricated

PHOTO BY JEREMY DILLON

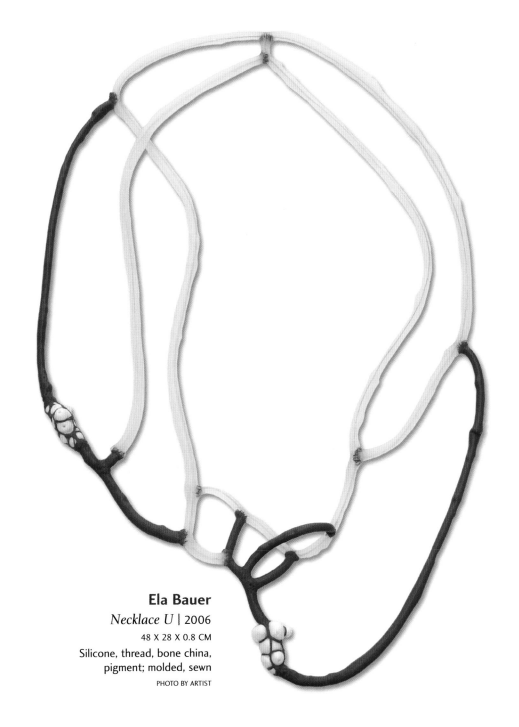

Ela Bauer

Necklace U | 2006

48 X 28 X 0.8 CM

Silicone, thread, bone china,
pigment; molded, sewn

PHOTO BY ARTIST

**Svetlana Rainous and
Youlia Rainous for alt&Go**

Ptolémée Duo Bracelet | 2004

7 X 8 X 4 CM

Gum, resin, colored brass;
hand fabricated, riveted

PHOTO BY ARTIST

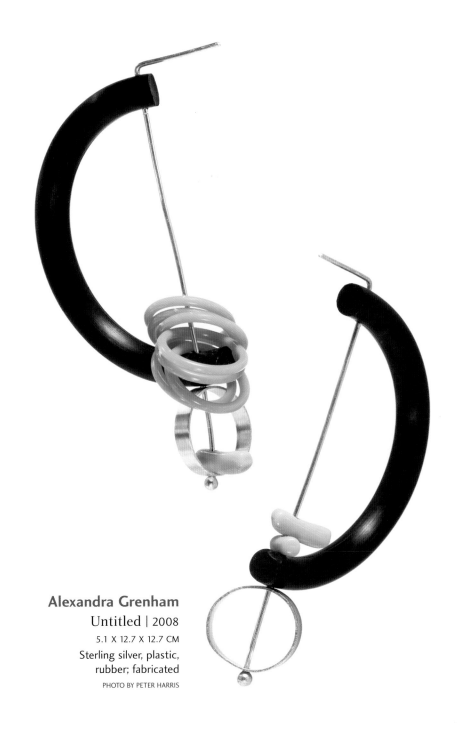

Alexandra Grenham
Untitled | 2008
5.1 X 12.7 X 12.7 CM
Sterling silver, plastic,
rubber; fabricated
PHOTO BY PETER HARRIS

Adam Paxon

*Squirming Rings
with Tails* | 2003

FRONT, 7.5 X 5.3 X 5.3 CM;
BACK, 7.8 X 5.5 X 5.5 CM

Acrylic; hand carved, polished

PHOTO BY GRAHAM LEES

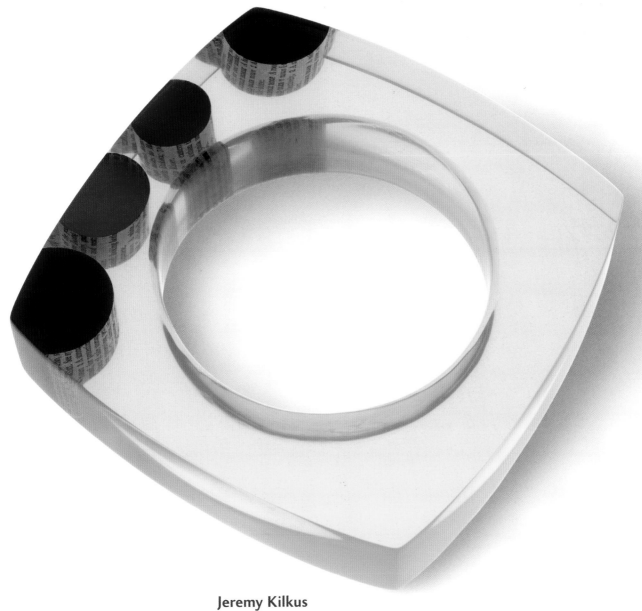

Jeremy Kilkus
Bracelet | 2007
10 X 10 X 2.5 CM
Resin, dictionary paper; carved
PHOTO BY RIK SFERRA

Sun-a Choi
Embracing Colors | 2008
24 X 14 X 0.9 CM
Sterling silver, cotton
thread, ribbon, plastic
PHOTO BY KWANG-CHOON PARK

Jaime Jo Fisher

Green Brooch | 2008

6.4 X 8.9 X 1.3 CM

Sterling silver, plastic, wool, thread; fabricated, sewn, stuffed, oxidized

PHOTO BY ROBERT BOLAND

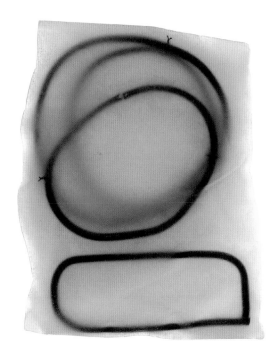

Coco Dunmire

A Lightness | 2008

11.5 X 9 X 2 CM

Resin, pigment, silver, iron, steel; hammered, hand fabricated

PHOTO BY FEDERICO CAVICCHIOLI

Niyati Haft

Heavy Load | 2007

CENTERPIECE, 6.1 X 10.3 X 0.6 CM;
CHAIN, 64.5 CM LONG

Plastic kite holder, iron chain,
sterling silver, epoxy cement;
fabricated, cold connected

PHOTO BY ARTIST

Jonathan Hernandez
Black Summer Ring Suite | 2007
LARGEST, 12.7 X 10.2 X 7.6 CM
Thermoplastic, silver,
aluminum, copper
PHOTO BY ROB GLOVER

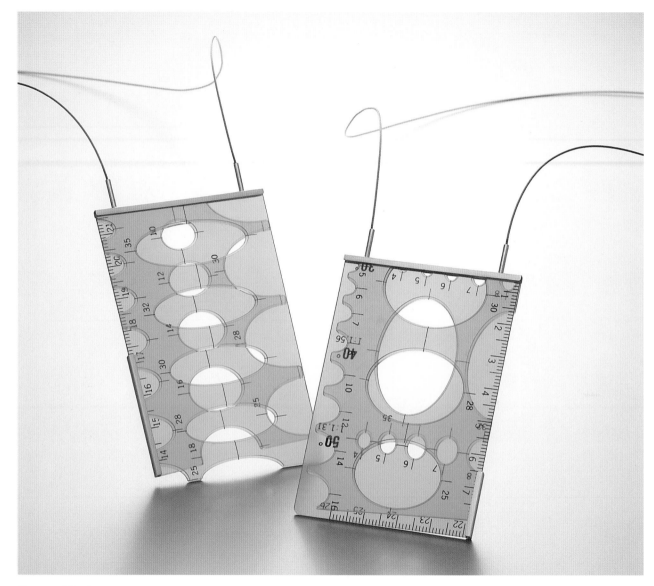

Sun-a Choi

Overlapped | 2007

LEFT, 8.5 X 5.5 X 0.3 CM
RIGHT, 8 X 5.3 X 0.3 CM

Sterling silver, plastic ruler

PHOTO BY KWANG-CHOON PARK

Maria Constanza Ochoa

Colour Bubbles | 2006

25 X 25 X 3.5 CM

Colored pencils, resin, sterling silver;
sawed, soldered, glued, fabricated

PHOTO BY SUNGHO CHO

emiko oye

My First Royal Jewels Jewellery Collection: The Duchess | 2008

26.7 X 24.8 X 6.4 CM

New and used Lego plastic, rubber cording;
hand fabricated, drilled, glued

Sang Min Lee
The Brooch Which Rotates | 2008
4.5 X 4.5 X 2.5 CM
Sterling silver, toy blocks,
bearing; fabricated, riveted
PHOTO BY STUDIO MUNCH

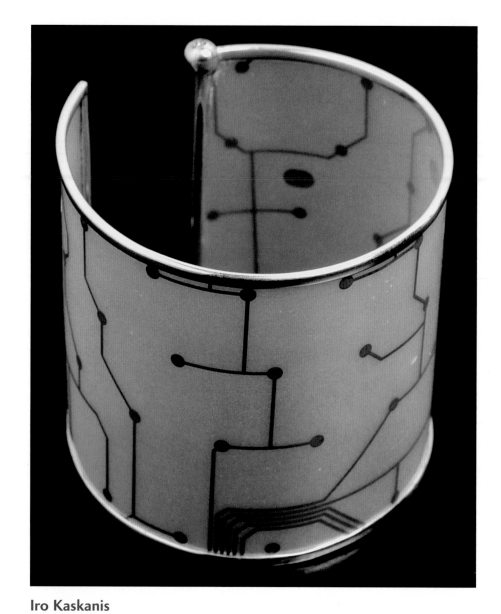

Iro Kaskanis

Hi-Tech | 2002

8.5 X 7 X 0.2 CM

Silver, polymer membrane;
hand fabricated

PHOTO BY DIMITRIS VATTIS

Philipp Spillmann

Ring! | 2008

3 X 3 X 1.4 CM

Sterling silver, plastic mobile
phone buttons; constructed

PHOTO BY ARTIST

Jung-a Noh

Keyboard Necklace | 2008

17.5 X 20.5 X 2 CM

Plastic keyboard, brass,
sterling silver, piano wire

PHOTO BY KWANG-CHOON PARK

Rebecca Strzelec

Mourning Bracelet 2 | 2008

11.5 X 11.5 X 10.2 CM

FDM plastic, baseball shell autographed
by Barry Bonds, waxed cotton cord;
rapid prototyped, CAD

PHOTO BY ARTIST

Fabrizo Tridenti
334 | 2007
12.5 X 7 X 2.7 CM
Recycled plastic, steel wire, electric
wire, moplen, correction fluid; glued
PHOTO BY ARTIST

Jocelyn Kolb

Heliotroph | 2008

38 X 38 X 7.5 CM

Gypsum, epoxy resin;
3D modeled, printed

PHOTO BY ARTIST

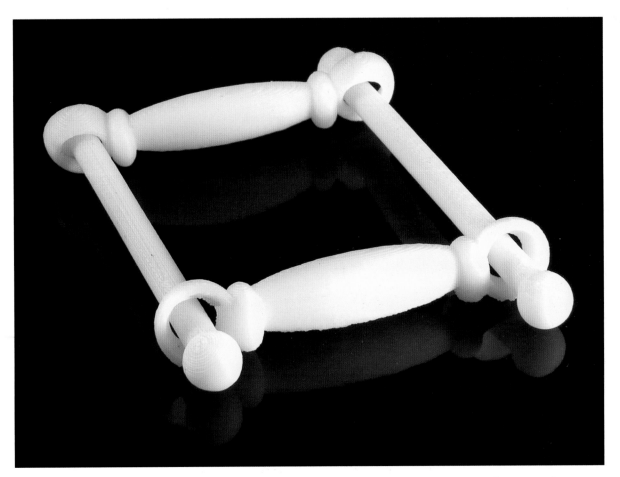

Sue Ann Dorman
The Slider Bracelet | 2007
7 X 9 X 2 CM
ABS white plastic; CAD/CAM
PHOTO BY ARTIST

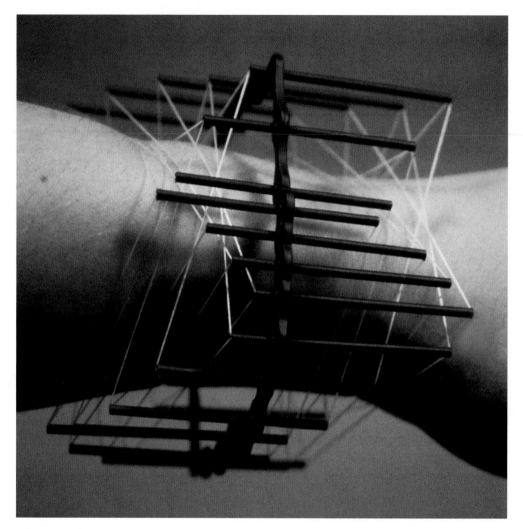

Alexia Cohen

Wrist Expansion 7 | 2006

10.2 X 8.9 X 6.4 CM

Brass frame, white elastic cord,
black paint; fabricated

Lily Yung

Planes Bracelet | 2007

11.4 X 11.4 X 5 CM

ABS plastic; rapid prototyped

PHOTO BY ARTIST

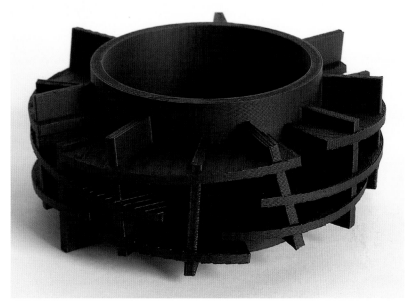

Lily Yung

Rings Necklace | 2007

25.4 X 21.6 X 1.9 CM

Photosensitive resin; rapid prototyped
by stereolithography

PHOTO BY ARTIST

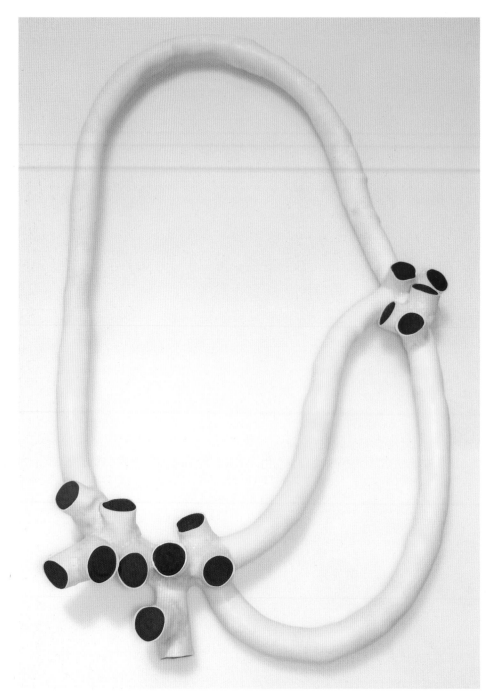

Ela Bauer
Necklace U | 2007
40 X 20 X 3 CM
Silicone, pigments;
molded, sewn
PHOTO BY ARTIST

Gail MacMillan-Leavitt
Babushka | 2007
19.4 X 15 X 9 CM
Limoges enamel, copper, thermoplastic acrylic resin, sterling silver, resin; cold connected
PHOTO BY ARTIST

Atelier Ted Noten

Turbo Princess | 1995

7.5 X 15 X 2.5 CM

Mouse with pearl necklace, acrylic,
silver, steel wire; cast, whitened

PHOTO BY ARTIST

Peter Deckers

Digital Division 1—Charles Babbage | 2001

3.3 X 2.9 X 0.3 CM

Sterling silver, digital print, acrylic; carved

PHOTO BY ARTIST

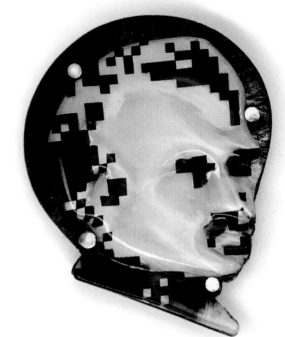

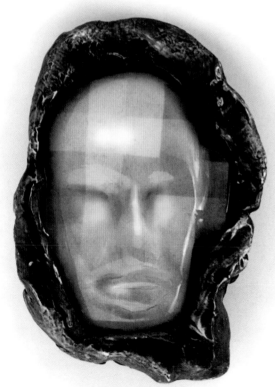

Peter Deckers

Digital Division 3—John van Neumann | 2001

4.3 X 3 X 0.6 CM

Sterling silver, digital print, acrylic; carved

PHOTO BY ARTIST

Felieke van der Leest
Meercat Don Q | 2006
10 X 4 X 5 CM
Plastic animal, textile, silver;
crocheted, metalsmithed
PHOTO BY EDDO HARTMANN

Monika Krol
Agrest (Gooseberry) | 2007
4.5 X 4.5 X 1 CM
Vintage plastic toy, sterling silver;
fabricated, bezeled, riveted
PHOTO BY KEN YANOVIAK

Peter Vermandere
Red Cloud Happiness (Brooch) | 2008
5.7 X 7.4 X 3.6 CM
Sterling silver, red lacquer, aluminum,
recycled plastic toy; mixed techniques
PHOTO BY SIGFRID EGGERG

Lonny Fechner

*The Collection of the
Satin Bowerbird* | 2007

1 X 100 X 100 CM

Wrapping paper, pendants; laminated

PHOTO BY FRANK KNUDSEN

The Satin Bowerbird is fond of blue stuff. The male uses blue found objects, including human trash, to decorate his bower, and the female chooses her mate based on how beautiful his place is. The habits of the bird inspired this piece. I made the pendants of blue stuff by laminating wrapping paper in the shapes of hearts and feathers. LF

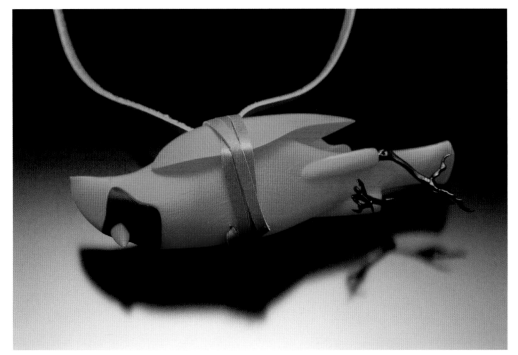

Rebecca Strzelec
Dead Cardinal for Dad 2 | 2008
7 X 19 X 6 CM
FDM plastic, pewter, paint, baseball-glove repair
leather; rapid prototyped, CAD, assembled
PHOTO BY ARTIST

Nicole Meyer

Flower Brooch | 2003

9 X 11 X 4.5 CM

Sterling silver, epoxy resin,
pigment; fabricated, inlaid

PHOTO BY PHIL DELLASEGA

Laura M.S. Brubaker
Grandma's Virginia Bluebell Earrings | 2007
EACH, 6.5 X 4.5 X 2 CM
Epoxy resin, pigment, sterling silver; cast,
forged, pierced, drilled, soldered
PHOTO BY ARTIST

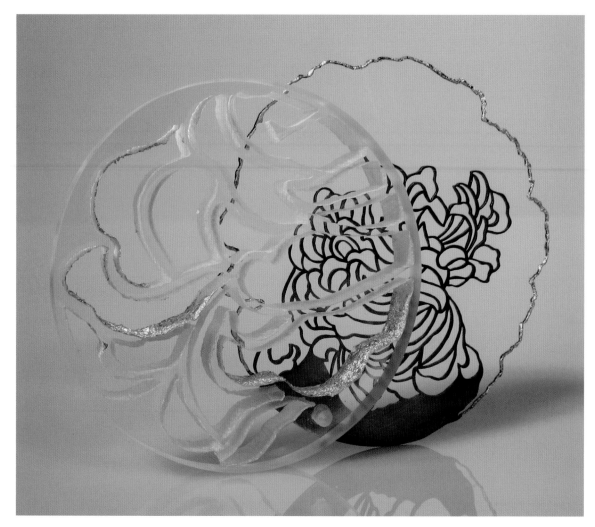

Vincent Pontillo

Pomegranate | 2008

10 X 10 X 1.3 CM

Acrylic, copper, 23-karat gold
leaf; pierced, riveted

PHOTO BY ARTIST

Sara Glaberson
Garden | 2005
3 X 4.3 X 0.8 CM
Mailing envelope, sterling silver,
glass, hair; embroidered
PHOTO BY ARTIST

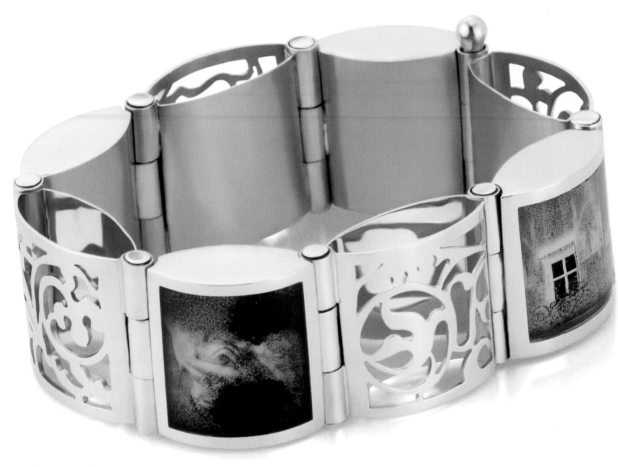

Linki van Zyl

Renaissance Bracelet | 2007

2 X 18 X 1.5 CM

Platinum, photographs by Johan Conradie, resin; hand fabricated, hand pierced, laminated

PHOTO BY KEVIN RUDHAM

Colleen Baran
Like Wearing a Love Letter Series: I Miss You | 2008
3.5 X 2.3 X 0.4 CM
Sterling silver, epoxy resin, rubber; hand fabricated
PHOTO BY ARTIST

Jantje Fleischhut
Bubble | 2007
9 X 6.5 CM
14-karat gold, epoxy,
print on foil
PHOTO BY ARTIST

Amy Tavern
In the Spring and Then Last Summer | 2005
5.1 X 3.8 X 2.5 CM
Sterling silver, resin,
chalk dust; fabricated
PHOTO BY HANK DREW

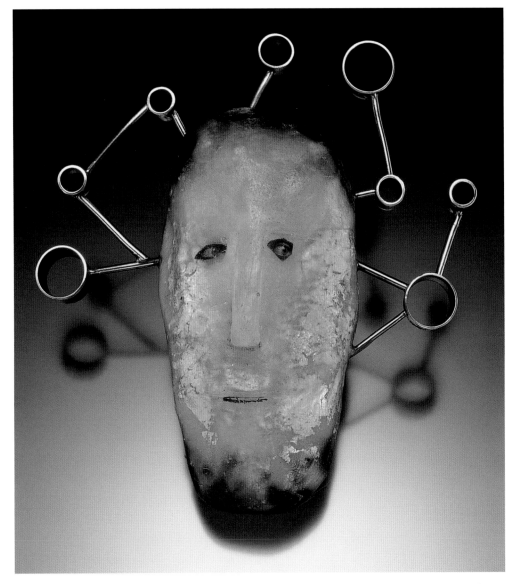

Susan Kasson Sloan
Head Brooch | 2004
8.9 X 9.5 CM
Epoxy resin, pigment, collage, 23-karat
gold leaf, sterling silver
PHOTO BY RALPH GABRINER

Silvia Weidenbach
Untitled | 2008
5.5 X 7 X 3 CM
Silver, plastic; cast,
installed, distorted
PHOTO BY UDO W. BEIER

Paula Crespo
Untitled (Necklace) | 2007
60 CM LONG; EACH PIECE, 6 X 3 CM
Vulcanized rubber, onyx,
gold; laser cut, fabricated
PHOTO BY JOÃO CARVALHO DE SOUSA

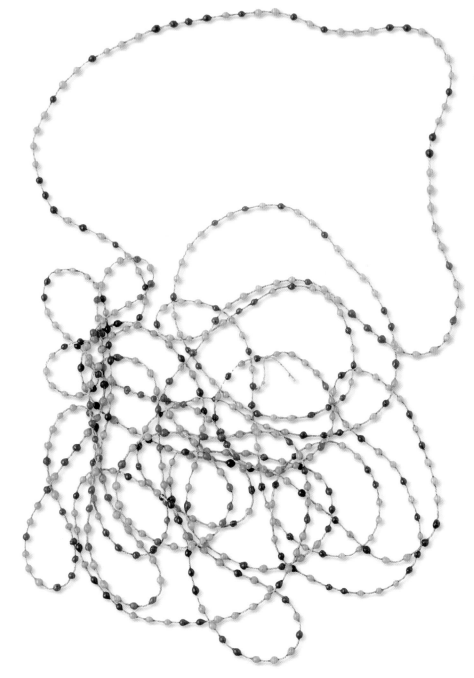

Nicole Lehmann

Necklace | 2006

438 CM IN LENGTH

Amber powder, epoxy
resin, hemp thread

PHOTOS BY UDO W. BEIER

Claudia Halder
Marmorkugel Ring | 2005
4 X 2.1 X 1.8 CM
Plastic; heat formed,
drilled, glued
PHOTO BY ARTIST

Michael Rossi
Untitled | 2008
2.5 X 7 X 1.3 CM
Sterling silver, nickel
silver, acrylic sheet
PHOTO BY JAMES OBERMEIER

Robert Dancik
*The Map Might Just Be
the Territory* | 2006
7.5 X 5.5 X 1.3 CM

Faux Bone, sterling silver, jasper, 14-karat
gold rivets, aquamarine, peridot,
amethyst; fabricated, scrimshawed

PHOTO BY DOUGLAS FOULKE

Eun Yeong Jeong

When the Dew Drops | 2005

VARIOUS DIMENSIONS

Artificial plastic marble, sterling silver;
filed, soldered, hand fabricated

PHOTO BY ARTIST

Emily Watson
Vena Cava Ring | 2008
4.8 X 2.2 X 1.6 CM
Bakelite, acrylic, brass,
epoxy; fabricated, carved
PHOTO BY ARTIST

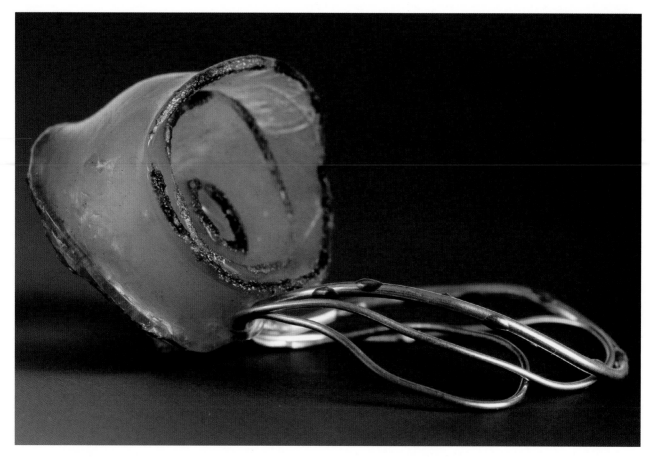

Mary Donald
Surfacing | 2008
2 X 2.5 X 6 CM
Latex, 18-karat gold,
Argentium silver; burned,
soldered, fabricated, riveted
PHOTO BY PATRICK LIOTTA

Karen J. Lauseng
Brooch | 1995

9 X 5.5 X 1 CM

Bleached cow bone, resin, sterling silver,
tree branches, agate; sliced, dyed, set, cast

PHOTO BY ARTIST

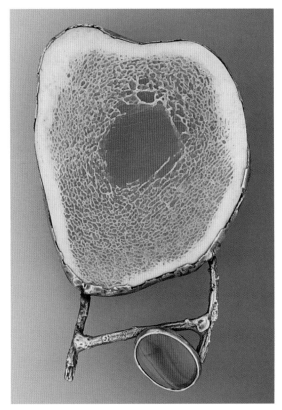

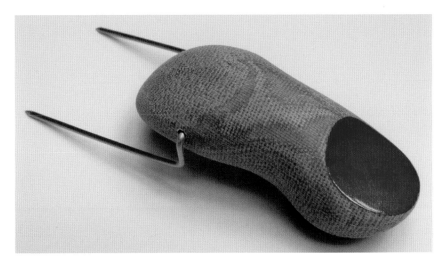

Birgit Laken
Fingerbrooch | 2006

4.5 X 2.3 X 2.1 CM

Phenol resin, fabric,
14-karat red gold

PHOTO BY ARTIST

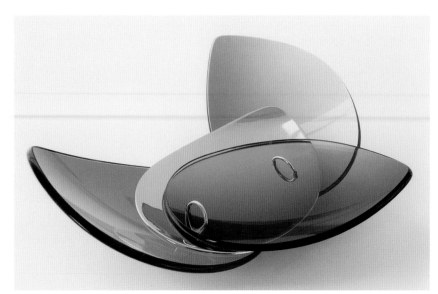

Jiro Kamata
Sunny Brooch | 2005
5 X 10 X 2 CM
18-karat gold, sunglasses,
silver; gold plated
PHOTO BY ARTIST

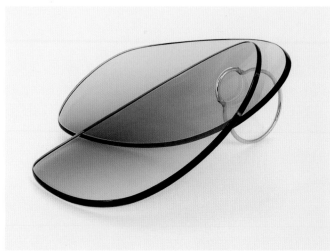

Jiro Kamata
Sunny Ring | 2005
4 X 6 X 3 CM
18-karat gold, sunglasses
PHOTO BY ARTIST

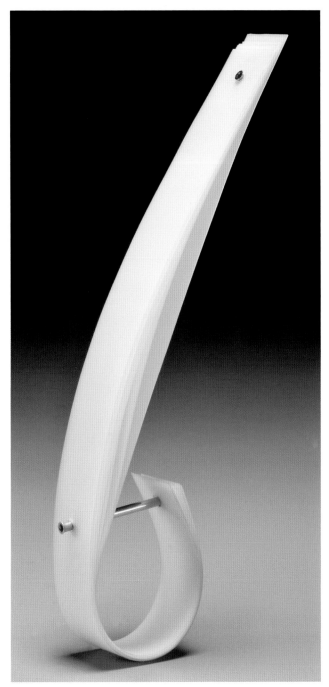

Lisa M. Johnson
Mylar Ring | 2008
10.1 X 1.9 X 1.9 CM
Polyester resin, 14-karat gold;
folded, riveted
PHOTO BY KEVIN MONTAGUE

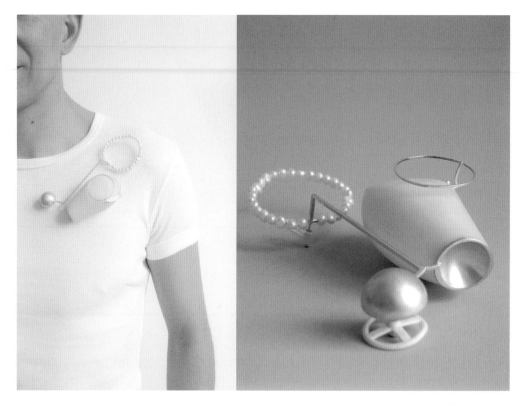

Jantje Fleischhut
Sateliten 2 Series: Altona 31, Salva, and Weisses | 2003
LARGEST, 4 X 5 X 9 CM
Found plastic, epoxy, fiberglass, silver,
pearls, found rubber, citrine
PHOTOS BY ARTIST

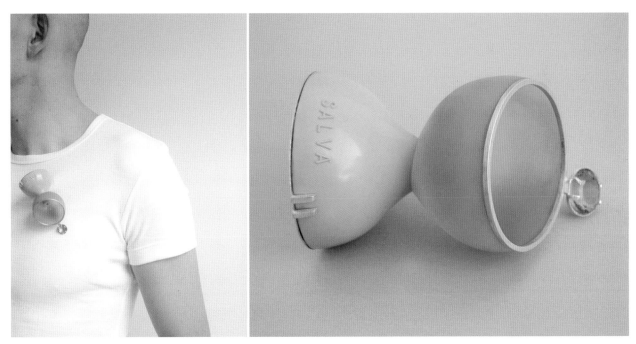

Katrin Veegen
Tranformation I–III (Set of Pins) | 2005
EACH, 6 X 5 X 1.5 CM
Resin, gold leaf, silver
PHOTO BY ARTIST

Karen McCreary
Nugget Bangle | 2008
8.5 X 9.5 X 3.5 CM
Polyester resin, 22-karat gold
leaf; cast, carved
PHOTO BY ARTIST

Jan Arthur Harrell

Sweet Sixteen Ring | 2007

18 X 15 X 15 CM

24-karat gold-plated copper, film,
plastic car taillight; fabricated

PHOTO BY JACK ZILKER

Eero Hintsanen
Red Carpet | 2007
2.5 X 7.3 X 0.9 CM
Sterling silver, foam rubber; hand
engraved, fabricated, gold plated
PHOTO BY CHAO-HSIEN KUO

Chris Jensen

Golden Lego Pendant | 2007

4.8 X 1.5 X 0.5 CM

Green Lego piece, 14-karat yellow gold,
diamonds, chrome diopside gemstones;
cut, cast, riveted, tube set

PHOTO BY ARTIST

Mary Donald
Recycling Bracelet | 2008
7.5 X 7.5 X 7.5 CM
Rubber, sterling silver, monofilament;
cut, fabricated, riveted
PHOTO BY PATRICK LIOTTA

Caroline Edwards

Gem Ring | 2008

3 X 4.4 X 2 CM

Epoxy resin, pigment; molded,
cast, sanded, polished

PHOTO BY JOSHUA HEARD

Geoff Riggle
Anamorphic Mother | 2008
23 X 15 X 15 CM
Polyester, acrylic lens,
motherboard, nickel silver, sterling
silver; laser cut, fabricated
PHOTO BY JEFFREY SABO

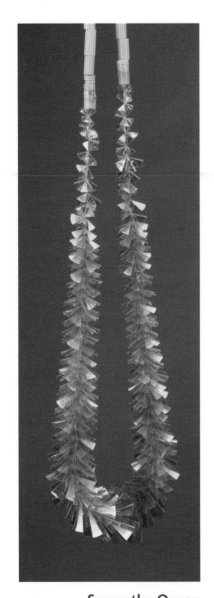

Samantha Queen

Green Lei Necklace | 2006

65 CM IN LENGTH

Plastic soda bottle;
scored, shaped

PHOTOS BY ARTIST

Christel van der Laan
The Price of Love (Brooch) | 2005

6 X 6.5 X 2.5 CM

Gold-plated sterling silver, polypropylene
swing tags; cut, dyed, woven, fabricated

PHOTO BY DOROTHY ERICKSON

Liana Kabel
Knitwit Bangles | 2005
EACH, 7.6 CM
Vintage knitting needles
PHOTO BY WAYNE KINGTON

Nicole Lehmann
Brooch | 2008
6.5 X 12 X 1 CM
Found plastic fragment,
14-karat gold; assembled
PHOTOS BY ARTIST

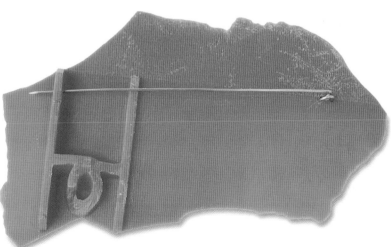

Karin Findeis

Garden Party (Amalgama) | 2008

4 X 5.5 X 5.5 CM

Sterling silver, plastic; fabricated

PHOTO BY BARRY LANGRISHE

Eun-ju Sim
Waves rise | 2008

LEFT, 5.9 X 5.7 X 3.2 CM;
RIGHT, 4 X 4.4 X 2.5 CM

Plastic file, sterling silver,
stainless steel; cut, riveted

PHOTO BY KC STUDIO

Suzanne Golden

Welcome to Hawaii | 2006

30 CM IN DIAMETER

Plastic beads, plastic tube; netted, angle stitched, woven

PHOTO BY ROBERT DIAMANTE

Minnette Walker

100's and 1000's Cross Pendant | 2007

Epoxy resin, candy sprinkles,
sterling silver; cast

PHOTO BY SARAH ROTHE

Annette Gerritse

Fantasy in PVC I | 2007

7 X 4 X 3 CM

Sterling silver, fine silver, fluorescent PVC,
suction cups, fluorescent acrylic beads,
nylon wire; pierced, filed, soldered, riveted

PHOTO BY M-WORKS

Karin Roy Michelle Andersson
You Want a Piece of Me? | 2008
RING, 6.5 X 4.5 X 3 CM; CAKE, 4 X 11 X 11 CM

Epoxy resin, paper, chili, salt,
coffee, textile, brass; glued

PHOTO BY ARTIST

Lilyana Bekic
Martha's Brass Knuckles | 2006
9.5 X 12.1 X 2.2 CM
Resin, fine silver, found objects, polymer
clay; cut, carved, riveted, fabricated

PHOTO BY ARTIST

Minnette Walker

Chocolate Brooch Series | 2007

VARIOUS DIMENSIONS

Polyester resin, pigment, oil paint,
almonds, nickel silver; cast

PHOTO BY SARAH ROTHE

Mina Kang

Ice Cream | 2008

VARIABLE DIMENSIONS

Silver, plastic spoons

PHOTO BY KWANG-CHOON PARK

Karen Fly
MelaMine Rings | 2007
EACH, 5 X 4 X 4 CM
Melamine; cut, carved
PHOTO BY STUART MCINTYRE

Karin Kato

A Snowy Street | 2006

19.8 X 6.5 X 1.3 CM

Sand, resin, silver; cast

PHOTO BY KOJI AIGA

Katja Prins

Machines Are US Series: Ring | 2004

3.5 X 2.5 X 3.5 CM

Silver, plastic

PHOTO BY EDDO HARTMANN

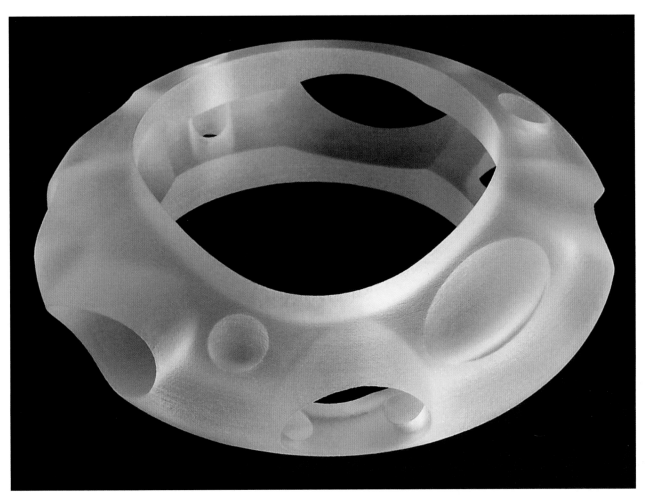

Lily Yung
HOBL-3C Bracelet | 2007
10.2 X 10.2 X 3.2 CM
Photosensitive resin; rapid
prototyped by stereolithography
PHOTO BY ARTIST

Jan Smith

Lion's Mane II | 2007

7.5 CM IN DIAMETER

Copper, nylon, monofilament, acrylic
plastic, sterling silver; anticlastic
raised, hand knotted, hand sawed

PHOTO BY DOUG YAPLE

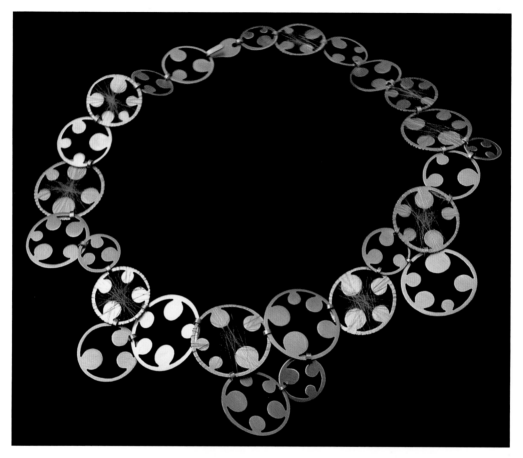

Ellie Boekman
Lunaria #1 (Neckpiece) | 2006
20 X 20 CM
Sterling silver, nylon thread
PHOTOS BY STEVE ROWE

Karen Bachmann

Carved Sphere Neck | 2006

50 X 3.8 CM

Clear acrylic, crystal beads, sterling
silver, silk; lathe turned, carved,
sandblasted, polished, strung

PHOTO BY ARTIST

Sabine Lang
Freestyle Bubbles Earrings | 2007
11 X 6 X 1 CM
Plastic, nylon, silver;
vacuum formed
PHOTO BY PER PEGELOW

Melinda Young
Neutral Bubble Rings | 2006
LARGEST, 5 X 4 X 0.3 CM
Acrylic; fabricated,
hand cut, finished
PHOTO BY ARTIST

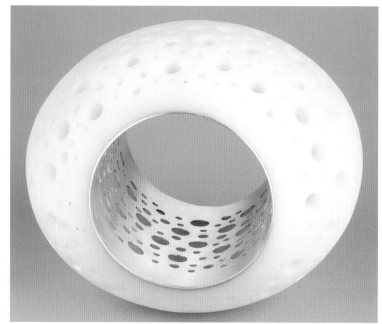

Sarah King
Untitled | 2005
11 X 13 X 10 CM
Bioresin, sterling silver; cast
PHOTO BY JEREMY JOHNS PHOTOGRAPHY

Jahyun Rita Baek
Cloud | 2007
25 CM IN DIAMETER
Acrylic, polymer
PHOTO BY STUDIO MUNCH

Brigitte Berndt
Endless Screw | 2007
4 X 4 X 4 CM
Nylon string, plastic, silver
PHOTO BY IMANIC GBR

Beate Weiss
Gavalon Black Net Ring | 2004
4 X 3 CM
Dental plastic, nylon net,
sterling silver
PHOTO BY PETRA JASCHKE

Sujin Park
Folding I | 2007
37 X 10 X 2.5 CM
Plastic sheet, plastic
beads; scored, folded
PHOTO BY MYUNG UK HUH

Karin Roy Michelle Andersson
Kotor | 2008
1 X 40 X 20 CM
Plastic, wood, pearl
silk; sawed, drilled, tied
PHOTO BY ARTIST

Body-Politics
Kathleen Taplick and Peter Krause
Singende Zelle | 2006

40 X 8 X 4.5 CM

Polyester, polyurethane, silver; constructed,
laminated, carved, melted

PHOTO BY HARTMUT BECKER

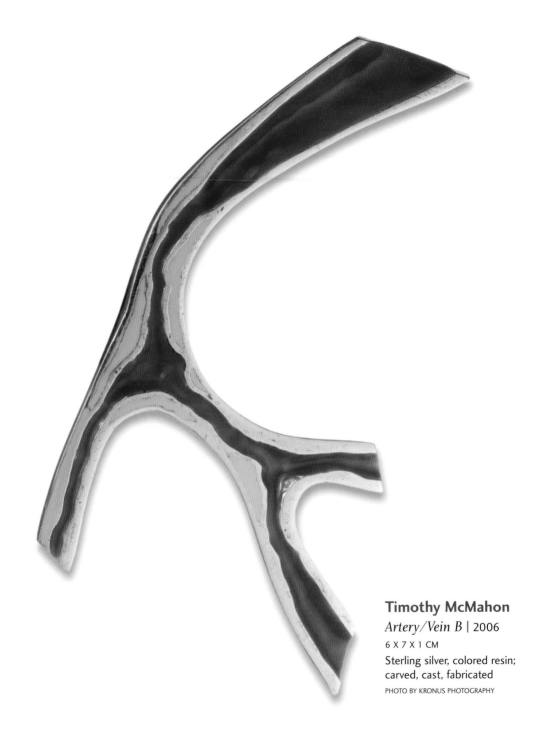

Timothy McMahon

Artery/Vein B | 2006

6 X 7 X 1 CM

Sterling silver, colored resin;
carved, cast, fabricated

PHOTO BY KRONUS PHOTOGRAPHY

Lisa Björke
Morbid Creature | 2007
30 X 6 X 6 CM
Epoxy resin, yarn, stone, silver, paper,
thermoplastic; crocheted, soldered
PHOTO BY ARTIST

Tanja Hartmann

BRC | 2008

EACH, 2 X 3 X 0.5 CM

Silicone

PHOTO BY STEFAN ZENKER

Coco Dunmire

Rambutan Red | 2008

5 X 6 X 4 CM

Recycled mesh bags, sponge, iron;
wrapped, sewn, hammered, formed

PHOTO BY FEDERICO CAVICCHIOLI

Jeongsuk Kwon
Strawberry | 2008
LARGEST, 3.5 X 2.2 X 1.9 CM
Epoxy resin, ceramics,
acrylic polymer
PHOTO BY KENJI UCHINO

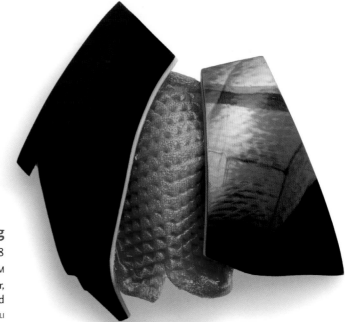

Marianne Casmore Denning
Vespa | 2008
11 X 12 CM
Thermoplastic, silver,
steel; fabricated
PHOTO BY FEDERICO CAVICCHIOLI

Vicki Mason

Leaf Hybrid | 2008

7.5 X 8.8 X 2 CM

Brass, copper, PVC, polyester
thread; powder coated, hand dyed,
cast, fabricated, cut, sewn, coiled

PHOTO BY TERENCE BOGUE

Kathryn Wardill

Standing Ring Series: Curved | 2006
LARGEST, 7 X 3 X 1 CM
Plastic, silver; hand carved
PHOTO BY ARTIST

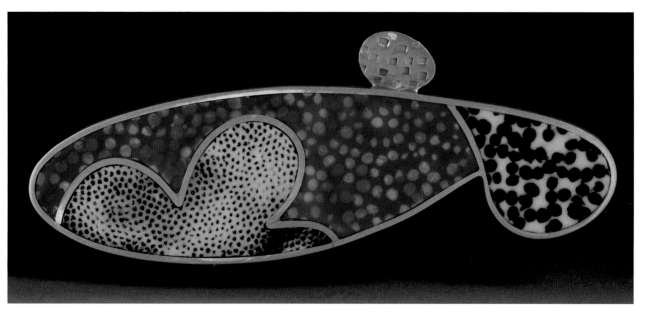

Robin Kraft
Lure Series: Brooch 2 | 2005
4 X 10 X 1 CM
Epoxy resin, sterling silver
PHOTO BY ARTIST

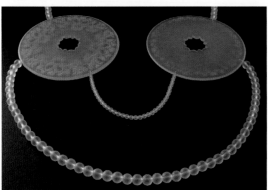

Birgit Laken

Summerland Series:
Disk Necklace | 2002

54 X 28 X 0.6 CM

Acrylic sheet, acrylic paint,
rock crystal; sprayed

PHOTOS BY ARTIST

Tracy Steepy

Both | 2006

80 X 28 X 1 CM

Acrylic polymer, sterling silver, epoxy resin; fabricated, laser cut, inlaid, hand drawn

PHOTO BY ARTIST

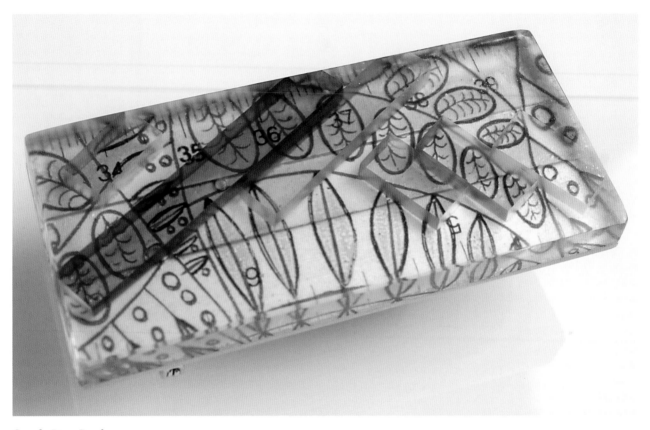

Sook Rye Park
The Color Sense | 2006
6.7 X 3.1 X 0.7 CM
Aluminum, acrylic, resin,
laser transfer paper
PHOTO BY TOMI

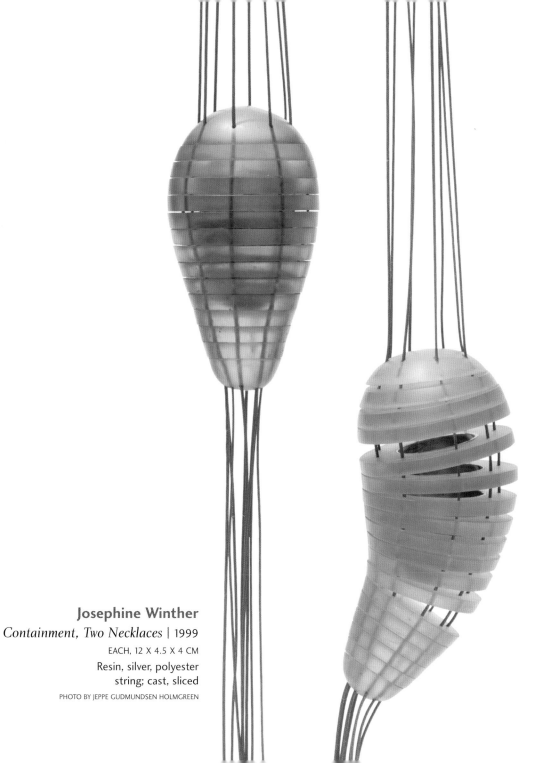

Josephine Winther
Containment, Two Necklaces | 1999
EACH, 12 X 4.5 X 4 CM
Resin, silver, polyester
string; cast, sliced
PHOTO BY JEPPE GUDMUNDSEN HOLMGREEN

Diane Falkenhagen
Red Upholstery Brooch | 2008
6.7 X 8.3 X 1.9 CM
Sterling silver, acrylic polymer;
fabricated, carved
PHOTO BY BILL POGUE

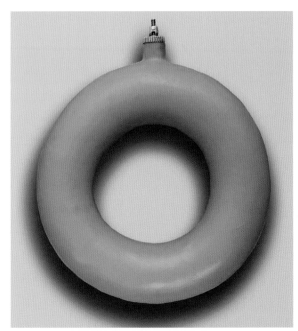

Katja Korsawe
Blow Up | 2000
10 X 3 CM
Latex, bicycle valve
PHOTO BY THOMAS SCHULTZE

Aud Charlotte Ho Sook Sinding

From the Vanitas Series | 2008

25 X 18 X 10 CM

Silicone, polyurethane plastic,
beads; hollow cast, flocked

PHOTO BY ARTIST

Natalya Pinchuk

Growth Series: Brooch | 2008

12 X 9 X 7 CM

Wool, copper, sterling silver, enamel, plastic fruit and flower parts, leather, waxed thread, stainless steel; fabricated, assembled

PHOTO BY ARTIST

Fabrizo Tridenti
Platform | 2007
5 X 3.3 X 2 CM
Epoxy resin, PVC tube, printed
circuit board; hand shaped
PHOTO BY ARTIST

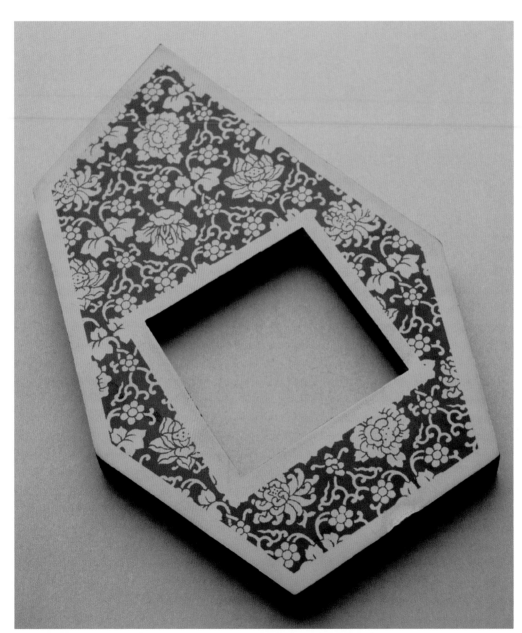

Hu Jun
Untitled | 2007
20.5 X 14 X 1.5 CM
Plastic, pigment; hand cut, printed
PHOTO BY ARTIST

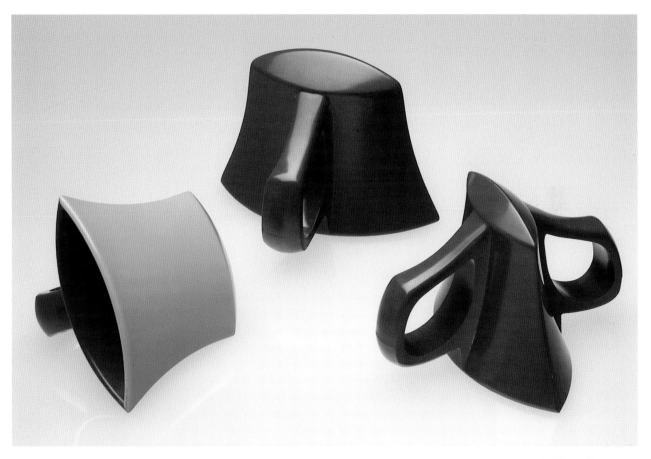

Sarah Kate Burgess
Two-Tone, Single, and Double | 2003
VARIOUS DIMENIONS
Found melamine cups, epoxy;
cut, sanded, finished
PHOTO BY BILL BACHHUBER

Katja Prins
Machines Are US Series: Ring | 2004
5.5 X 3 X 2.5 CM
Silver, plastic
PHOTO BY EDDO HARTMANN

Katja Prins
Flowerpiece #3 | 2006
8.5 X 5 X 3.5 CM
Silver, plastic
PHOTO BY EDDO HARTMANN

Jeanet Metselaar
Bracelet | 2006
5 X 11 X 3 CM
Plastic material
PHOTO BY BERT OTTEN

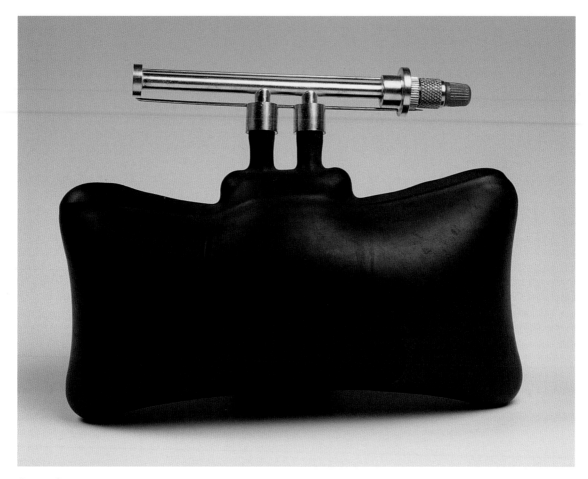

Sigurd Bronger
*Summerland Series:
Air Bag (Brooch)* | 2001
7 X 18 CM
Gold-plated brass,
steel, rubber
PHOTO BY ARTIST

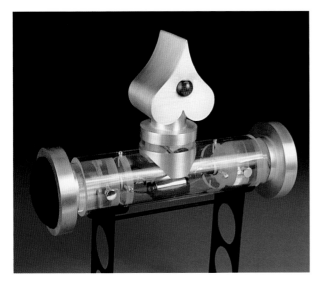

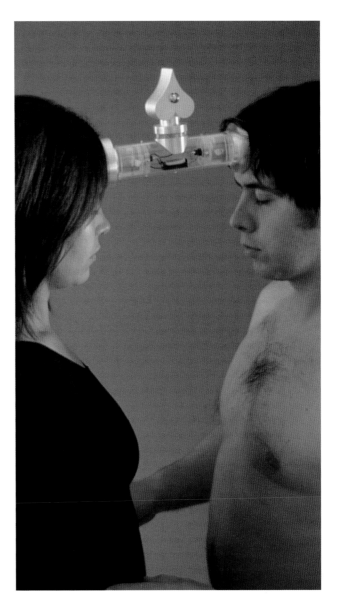

David Bausman
Ideas | 2005
20 X 15 X 7.5 CM
Sterling silver, acrylic, velvet;
mixed, hollow formed

MAIN PHOTO BY ARTIST
DETAIL PHOTO BY ROBLY GLOVER

Tzu-Ju Chen
Untitled (Bracelet) | 2005
48.3 X 15.2 X 7.6 CM
Foam, spray paint; fabricated
PHOTO BY TOMMY REYNOLDS

Sofia Björkman
Animals | 2008
5 X 3 X 2 CM
Styrene; vacuum formed
PHOTO BY ARTIST

Stevie B.

Don't | 2007–2008

14.6 X 5.4 X 1 CM

Sterling silver, brass, epoxy resin, pigment, patina, ribbon, photograph of Arlington National Cemetery; fabricated, stamped, soldered

PHOTO BY RALPH GABRINER

Shelby Ferris Fitzpatrick
Responsible Ring | 2006

8 X 10.5 X 6 CM

Polyurethane, laminated paper, computer-
printed text, images from open-pit mining
operations; pierced, laminated, shaped

PHOTOS BY ARTIST

Leslie Shershow
Untitled (Brooch) | 2008
7.5 X 6 X 0.5 CM
Sterling silver, thermoplastic,
wood; fabricated, cast
PHOTO BY JOHN SNEDEN

Leslie Shershow
Untitled (Brooch) | 2008
11.5 X 6.5 X 1 CM
Sterling silver, thermoplastic,
coral; fabricated
PHOTO BY JOHN SNEDEN

Mona Wallstrom

Spirit Brooch | 2006

9 X 7 X 4 CM

Acrylic, rubber, copper;
hand milled, constructed

PHOTO BY ARTIST

Coco Dunmire

Riscaldamento | 2008

45 X 8.5 X 2.5 CM

Resin, pigment, fine silver, cord;
hammered, hand fabricated

PHOTO BY FEDERICO CAVICCHIOLI

Sarah King
Untitled | 2001
3.5 X 39 X 1.5 CM
Bioresin, sterling silver;
cast, oxidized
PHOTO BY JEREMY JOHNS PHOTOGRAPHY

Alexandra Chaney
Repel: Aprilophobia | 2007
36 X 36 X 9 CM
Monofilament fishing line, pink yarn, epoxy, clear
plastic hose, polyurethane hub syringe needles,
syringe plunger tips; knitted, sewn, tension set

PHOTO BY JUSTIN COLT BECKMAN

Yuh-Shyuan Chen
Web | 2006
23 X 14.5 X 2 CM
Copper, latex; fabricated
PHOTO BY ARTIST

Masumi Kataoka
Untitled | 2008
13 X 7.5 X 5 CM
Rawhide, liquid plastic,
sterling silver, nickel,
pigment; fabricated,
coated, filed
PHOTO BY ARTIST

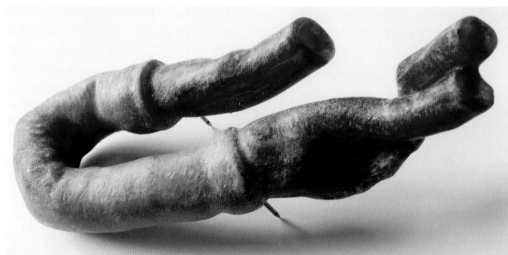

Hsi-Hsia Yang
Web | 2005
3 X 50 X 30 CM
Sterling silver, vinyl;
fabricated, riveted, cast
PHOTO BY ARTIST

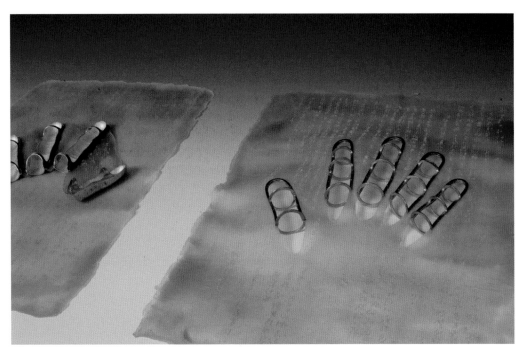

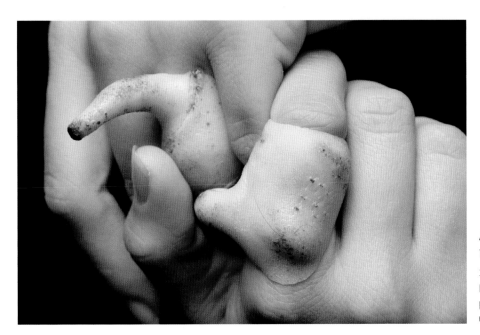

Anna Logunova
Untitled | 2007
3 X 4 X 6 CM
Rubber, glue,
pigment; burnt
PHOTO BY ARTIST

Mary McMullen
Digitorium | 2005
6 X 4 X 2 CM
Epoxy resin, cosmetics, pigments
PHOTO BY TOM MCINVAILLE

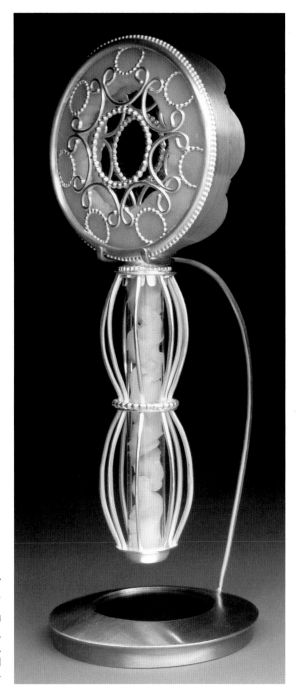

Jill K. Baker Gower
Flesh Vanity Brooch | 2007
10.5 X 4.5 X 3.5 CM
Sterling silver, convex mirror,
silicone rubber, glass test tube,
monofilament; fabricated
PHOTO BY ARTIST

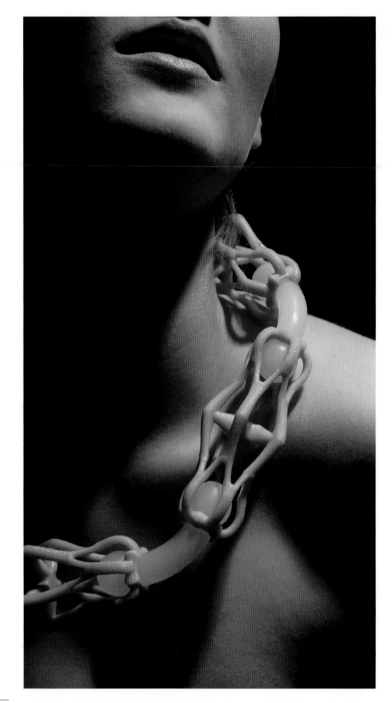

Anthony Tammaro
Lattice Two | 2008
30 X 30 X 5 CM
Gypsum, epoxy resin,
silicone rubber
PHOTOS BY ADAM WALLACAVAGE

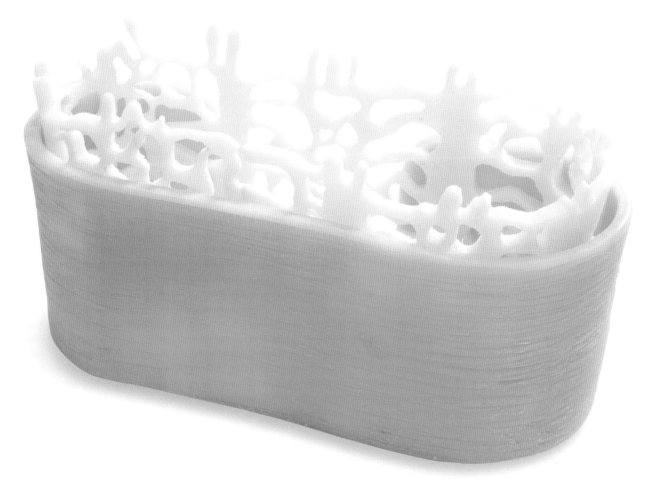

Javier Moreno Frias
Mesh | 2007
10.1 X 5.1 X 4 CM
Gold, silver, plastic,
paint; fabricated
PHOTO BY ARTIST

Anthony Tammaro

Neck Object One | 2008

33 X 33 X 10 CM

Gypsum, epoxy resin,
silicone rubber

PHOTO BY ADAM WALLACAVAGE

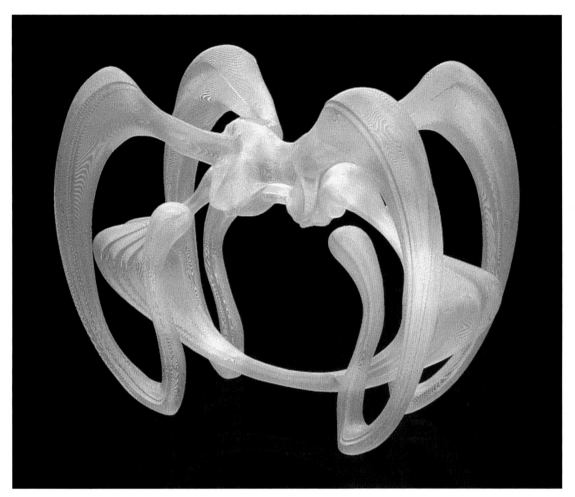

Jennifer Theokary
Intrusion #2 | 2006
8.1 X 9.4 X 5.6 CM
SLA epoxy resin;
rapid prototyped
PHOTO BY ARTIST

Kaori Watanabe
Tikki, Tikki (Necklace) | 2003
LENGTH, 72 CM
Sterling silver, fluorescent
thermoplastic
PHOTO BY FEDERICO CAVICCHIOLI

Ineke Otte
Necklace Chunk | 2004
20 X 20 X 2 CM
Resin, brass
PHOTO BY ARTIST

Svenja John
Altai Bracelet | 2006
11 X 6 CM
Surface-treated polycarbonate;
water jet colored and cut
PHOTO BY TIVADAR NEMESI

Ruudt Peters

Azoth 40 | 2005

6.8 X 4.5 X 2.2 CM

Silver, polyester

PHOTO BY ARTIST

Nicole Polentas

Anopolis Ring | 2008

7 X 6 X 5 CM

Sterling silver, copper, thermoplastic, pigment; fused, fabricated

PHOTO BY JEREMY DILLON

Karin Kato
QU4DRO | 2006
LARGEST, 5.5 X 5.2 X 1.1 CM
Sand, resin, silver; cast
PHOTO BY ARTIST

Babette Von Dohnanyi
Untitled | 2005
EACH, 1.5 X 2 X 2 CM
Crystal, sterling silver,
resin; cast, soldered
PHOTO BY FEDERICO CAVICCHIOLI

Sandra Zilker

Pin Series: Donuts with Tails | 2006

EACH, 9.5 X 2.5 X 0.5 CM

Sterling silver, epoxy resin, marker, acrylic; fabricated, laminated, inlaid

PHOTO BY JACK B. ZILKER

Peter Chang
Untitled Bracelet | 2005
15.3 X 15.3 X 5.2 CM
Acrylic, PVC, found plastic, silver; thermoformed,
carved, lathe turned, polished
PHOTO BY ARTIST

Jaime Jo Fisher

Strawberry Tiered Pillow Bracelet | 2008

20.3 X 4.5 X 1.9 CM

Sterling silver, recycled plastic, polyester fiberfill, thread; fabricated, sewn, stuffed, strung

PHOTO BY ROBERT BOLAND

Tracy Page Smith
PopArt Bracelet | 2006
2.2 X 17.5 X 0.4 CM
Sterling silver, resin;
hand pigmented
PHOTO BY DANIEL W. SMITH

Nisa Blackmon

ZBSS.JL.01, Neckpiece with
005.5 Section Array | 2007

28 X 30 X 23 CM

Plastic flowers, plasticized paint, aluminum, acrylic resin, sterling silver; dissected, recombined, tagged, dipped, embedded, sectioned, fabricated, riveted, tagged

PHOTOS BY ARTIST

Amy McColl

Gingko Ring Series | 2007

EACH, 2 X 4 X 3 CM

Silver, resin, glitter, spray
paint; saw pierced, oxidized

PHOTO BY ARTIST

Caroline Cowen

Flower Necklace | 2008

5 X 10 X 1.5 CM

Sterling silver, epoxy resin;
saw pierced, patterned, inlaid

PHOTO BY ARTIST

Velina A. Glass
Out of Africa | 2008
6.5 X 9.5 X 4 CM
Epoxy resin, transparency
paper, color pigments; cast
PHOTO BY ARTIST

Pirada Senivongse Na Ayudhya
Untitled | 2005
23 CM IN DIAMETER
Acrylic, silver, fabric; hand dyed,
laser cut, hand woven
PHOTO BY VISIONARY

Minna Karhu
Picked One Brooch | 2007
12.3 X 7.1 X 7.4 CM
Recycled plastic, silver, steel;
heat shaped, riveted
PHOTO BY ARTIST

Andi Velgos
Fireflies (Bracelet) | 2007
6 X 9 X 9 CM
Rubber, crystals, steel wire
PHOTO BY ARTIST

Fran Allison
Rearranging Nature | 2008
9.5 X 6 X 2.5 CM
Sterling silver, polyester resin,
paint; cast, fabricated
PHOTO BY ARTIST

Hsi-Hsia Yang
Unwithered Flower | 2005
15 X 15 X 50 CM
Vinyl; cast
PHOTO BY ARTIST

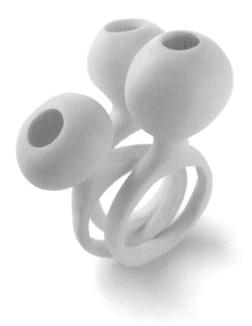

Kathryn Wardill

White Pod Series (Bracelet, Brooch, and Three Rings) | 2007

BRACELET, 12 X 8 X 3 CM;
BROOCH, 8 X 3 X 2 CM;
EACH RING, 3 X 3 X 1.5 CM

Plastic, silver, steel; hand carved

PHOTOS BY ARTIST

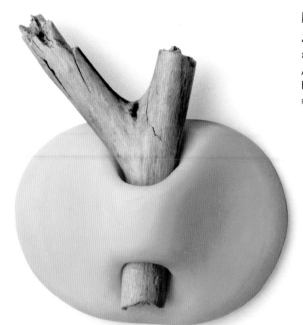

Mona Wallstrom
Saved Brooch | 2006
8 X 7 X 2 CM
Acrylic, wood, silver;
hand milled
PHOTO BY ARTIST

Sofia Björkman
Wanna Be Precious | 2005
12 X 3 X 2 CM
Plastic flooring,
carpet; vacuum formed
PHOTO BY ARTIST

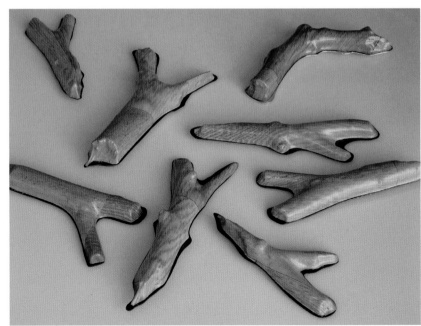

Iris Bodemer

Untitled Neckpiece | 2004

40 X 30 X 1 CM

Plastic, 18-karat gold,
quartz, pearls, tape

PHOTO BY JULIAN KIRSCHLER

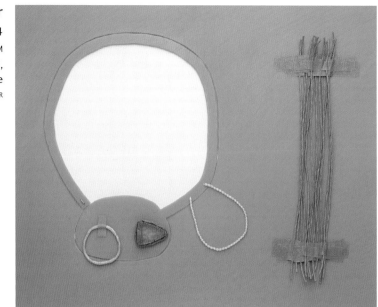

Iris Bodemer

Untitled Neckpiece | 2000

46 X 12 X 1.5 CM

Silver, magnesite, plastic

PHOTO BY JULIAN KIRSCHLER

Ela Bauer

Necklace U | 2005

40 X 8 X 2 CM

Silicone; cast, molded, sewn

PHOTO BY ARTIST

Alidra Alić Andre de la Porte
Tulip | 2008
10 X 7 CM
Sterling silver, resin, plastic, tulip flower
PHOTO BY DORTE KROGH

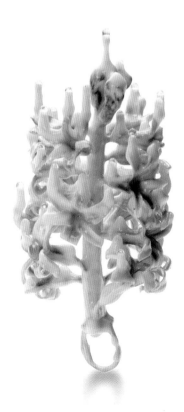

Alidra Alić Andre de la Porte
Hyacinth | 2008
17 X 8 CM
Sterling silver, resin, plastic, strawberry quarts, hyacinth flower
PHOTO BY DORTE KROGH

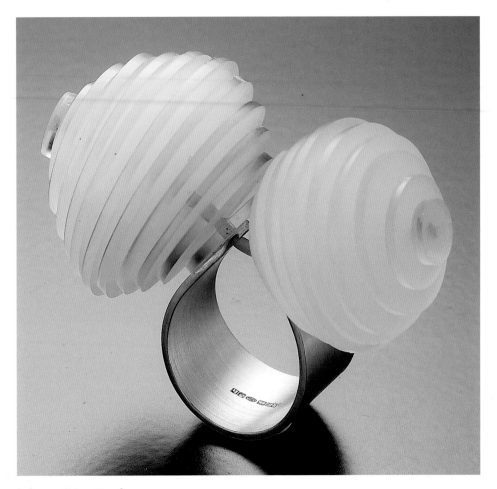

Jahyun Rita Baek
Cloud | 2007
3 X 3 X 1.5 CM
Sterling silver, acrylic, polymer
PHOTO BY STUDIO MUNCH

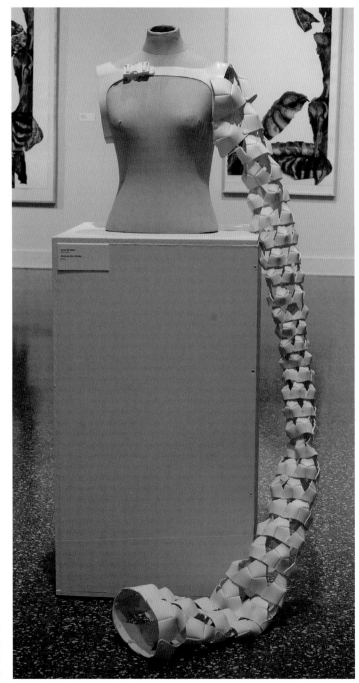

Jung Ah Hahn
Modular Arm Girdle | 2007
188 X 43 X 20 CM
Reused plastic, polyethylene
foam; heat formed, stitched
PHOTO BY THOMAS HILTON

Gitte Nygaard

Opus Formosus Collection: Reginae Culina Scapium | 2004–2005

13 X 11.5 CM

Thermoplastic polyurethanes,
ready-made plastic bowl; cut

PHOTO BY JOSIE SYKES

Lauren N. Pineda

Moth Necklace | 2007

NECKLACE, 43.5 CM IN LENGTH; WINGS, 7 X 5 CM

Sterling silver, polyurethane
resin, powder pigment,
crystals; fabricated, inlaid

PHOTO BY ANDREY CHEPUSOV

Teresa Faris
Neckpiece #2 | 2004
25.4 X 1.9 CM
Latex, sterling silver; painted
PHOTO BY ARTIST

Alexis Pierre-Louis
Lot's Wife (Ring) | 2008
8 CM IN LENGTH
Thermoset PVC, salt,
polyurethane, oil paint
PHOTO BY ARTIST

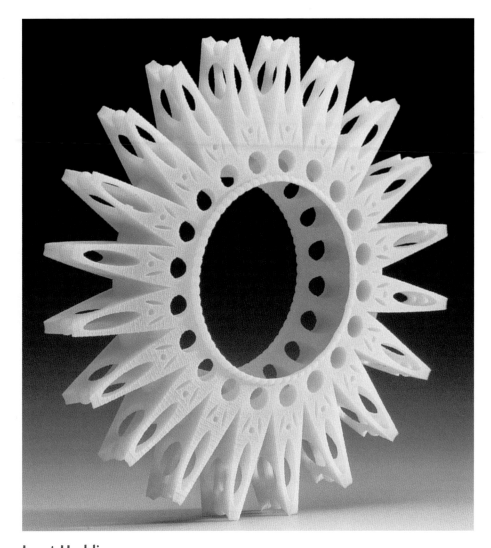

Janet Huddie

Isambard's Bracelet #1 | 2008

3 X 6.5 X 15 CM

Duraflex photopolymer;
computer-assisted rapid prototyped

PHOTO BY JOSEPH HYDE

Billie Jean Theide
Carat Bracelet | 2008
BRACELET, 7 CM IN DIAMETER;
EACH DIAMOND, 3 X 5 CM
High-density polyethylene milk jugs,
hard fiber washers; dyed, fabricated
PHOTO BY ARTIST

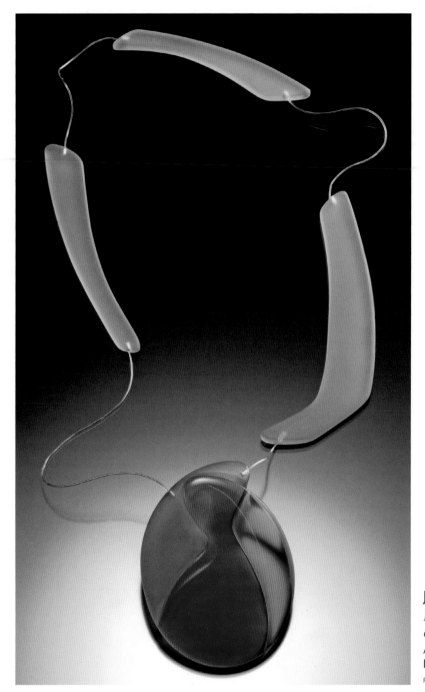

Jennifer Shaline
Polaris | 2006
6.4 X 0.6 CM
Acrylic sheet, rubber cord;
laminated, hand carved
PHOTO BY LARRY SANDERS

Estefânia R. De Almeida
Anthropology (Pin) | 2007
EACH, 1.9 X 0.8 CM
Bakelite, steel; hand sawed
PHOTO BY CARMEN GRAÇA

Liana Kabel
Knitwit Necklace | 2007
43.2 CM
Vintage knitting needles, stainless
steel, enamel, sterling silver
PHOTO BY ARTIST

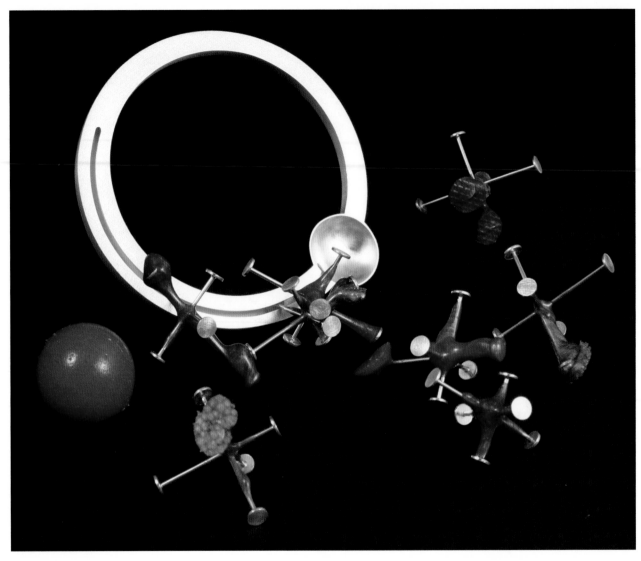

Jennifer Wehlacz
Jill Plays Jack | 2008
10 X 10 X 4 CM
Sterling silver, polyurethane rubber,
magnets; fabricated, cast, poured
PHOTO BY ARTIST

Melinda Alexander
Puzzle | 2007
2.5 X 45.7 CM
Resin, sterling silver, pearls,
diamonds; fabricated
PHOTO BY ROB ROMEO

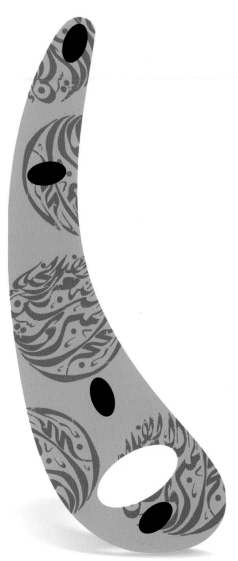

Essor

Lussy Bracelet | 2004

7 X 7 X 7 CM

Transparent film, self-adhesive
layering; hand fabricated

PHOTOS BY ARTIST

Iris Weyer

Pop-Ups | 2006

TALLEST, 10 X 6 X 0.5 CM

Clothespins, acrylic; jet
cut, rapid prototyped

PHOTOS BY DIRK WEYER

Edward Lane McCartney
Vaseline Necklace | 2006
4 X 20 X 20 CM
Acrylic sheet, sterling
silver; heat formed
PHOTO BY JACK B. ZILKER

Camille Borbouse
Untitled | 2008
EACH, 5.6 X 0.3 CM
Acrylic, epoxy;
thermally formed
PHOTO BY ARTIST

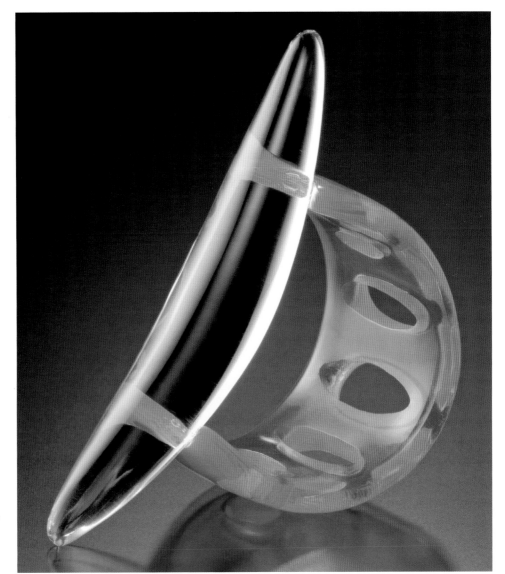

I made the Taurus ring so that it can be worn two different ways. The clear portion of the ring can rest on the top of the fingers, or it can be grasped in the hand. JS

Jennifer Shaline

Taurus | 2006

3.2 X 3.8 X 1.3 CM

Ultraviolet light-sensitive acrylic; fabricated, heat formed, fused, carved

PHOTO BY LARRY SANDERS

Pavel Herynek

Plastic Nature Series: Bracelet | 2004

9.5 X 8.5 X 6 CM

Plastic; hand fabricated

PHOTO BY MARKÉTA ONDRUŠKOVÁ

Gill Forsbrook
Untitled | 2004
15 X 13 X 3 CM
Polypropylene, polycarbonate,
silver; hand fabricated
PHOTO BY ARTIST

Barbara Cohen
Untitled | 2007
16 X 16 X 2.5 CM
Nylon mesh, foam rubber, sterling silver,
freshwater pearls; oxidized, fabricated
PHOTO BY ARTIST

Sofia Calderwood
Blue Frond Bracelet | 2006
15 X 15 X 7.5 CM
Plastic tubing, silver leaf, cable
ties; crocheted, heat shrunk, dyed
PHOTO BY ARTIST

Colleen Baran

Like Wearing a Love Letter Series: You See Me | 2007

3.4 X 4.7 X 4.5 CM

Polycarbonate, sterling silver, archival ink, resin,
thread; hand fabricated, sewn, crocheted

PHOTO BY ARTIST

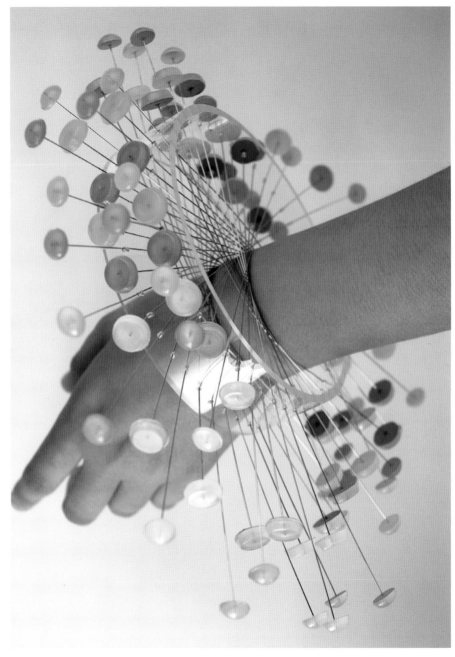

Elsa Perez
Order/Chaos Bracelet B | 2008
26 X 26 X 3.5 CM
Acrylic, guitar string, vinyl, paper;
fabricated, assembled
PHOTO BY EUGENE MONNIER III

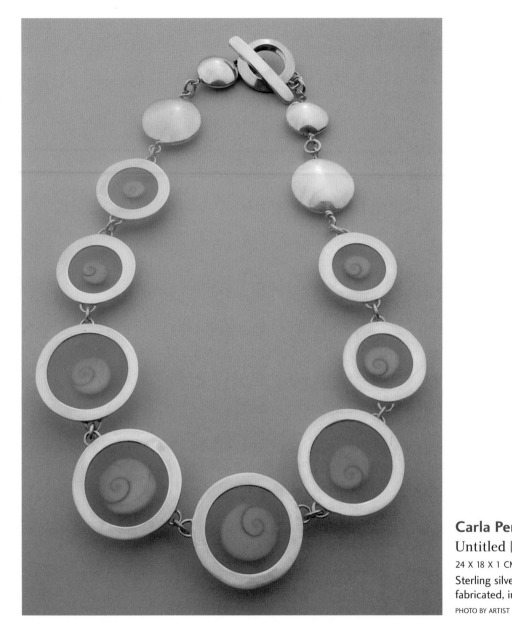

Carla Pennie McBride

Untitled | 2008

24 X 18 X 1 CM

Sterling silver, epoxy resin, shell; fabricated, inlaid

PHOTO BY ARTIST

Dania Chelminsky
Untitled | 2007
EACH, 11 X 2.5 X 3 CM
Epoxy resin, egg shells;
molded, cast, hand
carved, finished
PHOTO BY RAN ERDE

Fabienne Vuilleumier
Untitled | 2007
2.5 X 2 X 1 CM
Medical plastic, plastic
pearls; thermoformed
PHOTO BY ARTIST

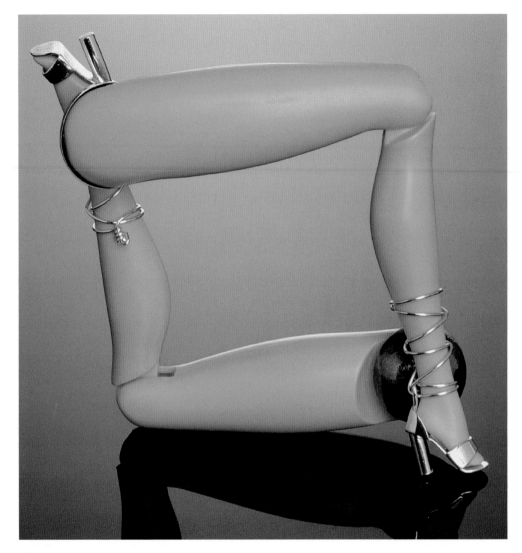

Margaux Lange

Silver Shoes Bracelet | 2005

8.9 X 10.2 X 2.5 CM

Sterling silver, plastic doll legs, patina;
hand fabricated, assembled

PHOTO BY QUADPHOTO-SARATOGA, MARK VAN AMBURGH

Aram Choi

Saturation | 2006

3.5 X 11 X 6.5 CM

Sterling silver, plastic,
dolls, candy

PHOTOS BY ANGIE PONSO

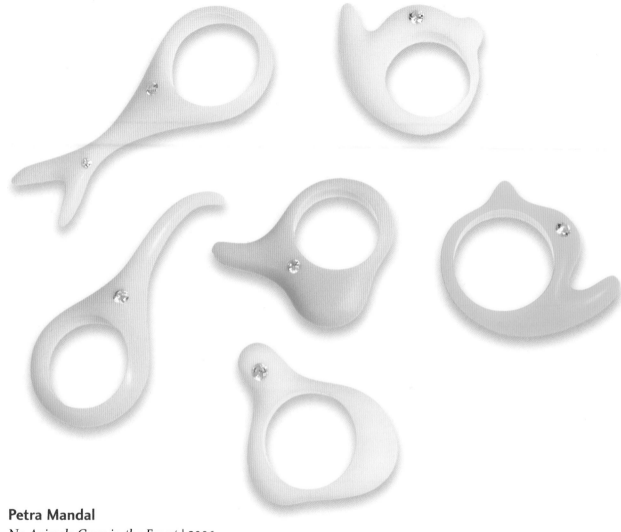

Petra Mandal

No Animals Grow in the Forest | 2006

EACH, 3.8 X 2.5 X 7 CM

Acrylic, cubic zircon

PHOTO BY STEFAN JOHANSSON

Gitte Nygaard

Domestic Collection: Handyrabbits | 2005–2006

LARGEST, 7 X 4.5 CM

Thermoplastic polyurenthanes, silver; cut

PHOTO BY PATXI CALVO

Amy McColl

Gladioli Bangle | 2007

6 X 12 CM

Thermoplastic, resin

PHOTO BY ARTIST

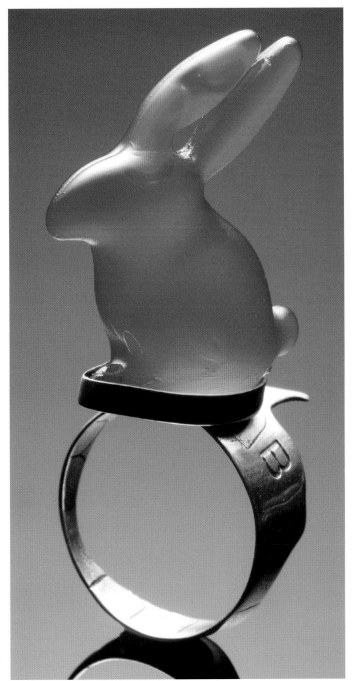

Kandice Mascotti
Bunny Ring | 2007
5.7 X 3.2 X 2.5 CM
Bunny bath bead,
sterling silver
PHOTO BY PETER LEE

Nazan Pak

Eleven-Rose Necklace | 2004

18 X 2.7 CM

Epoxy resin, pigment;
cast, hand fabricated

PHOTO BY ELA CINDORUK

Melinda Young

Green Fingers Rings | 2008

LARGEST, 4 X 2.5 X 0.3 CM

Acrylic; fabricated,
hand cut, finished

PHOTO BY ARTIST

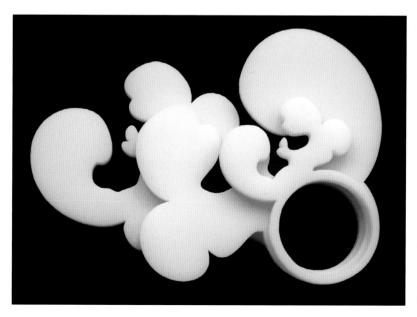

Elizabeth Boyd Hartmann

Untitled | 2008

5 X 8 X 0.8 CM

Acrylic; laser cut

PHOTO BY ARTIST

Aimee A. Domash

Spring Has Sprung | 2007

6 X 3.5 X 0.7 CM

Plastic, polypropylene, gold pen, vellum, Argentium wire,
pearls, glass disks; cut, riveted, hammered, embellished

PHOTO BY SALMON ROCK STUDIO

Suzanne Golden
Bauble-Licious | 2007
33 CM IN DIAMETER
Plastic beads, seed beads;
angle stitched, woven, strung
PHOTO BY ROBERT DIAMANTE

Ineke Otte
Necklace Green As Grass | 2005
25 X 25 X 5 CM
Plastic
PHOTO BY ARTIST

Ami Avellán
Eldorado | 2007
28 X 9 X 1.4 CM
Reflector, plastic buttons, sterling silver, fire opal,
pearls, silk, stainless steel needle; engraved
PHOTO BY ARTIST

Christine Harwart
Plastiflor Pin Rounds | 2006
EACH, 4.5 X 2 CM
PVC, nylon, sterling silver;
hand cut, sawed
PHOTO BY PETRA JASCHKE

Christine Harwart
Plastiflor Ring | 2006
2.5 X 2.5 X 2.5 CM
PVC, nylon; hand cut, sawed
PHOTO BY PETRA JASCHKE

Sarah Keay
Pink Bangle | 2006
15 X 15 X 3 CM
Silver, plastic, monofilament, enamel;
bobbin knitted, hand fabricated
PHOTO BY ARTIST

Shawn C. Smith

Collaborative Pendant | 2008

9 X 5 X 4 CM

Sterling silver, rubber, hot glue; fabricated

PHOTO BY ARTIST

Seainin Passi
Hot-Melt Glue Neckpiece | 2007
40 X 10 CM
Embroidery thread, ethylene-vinyl acetate
PHOTO BY RICHARD BOLL PHOTOGRAPHY

Chequita Nahar
Seeds (Ring) | 2007
4.1 X 2.8 X 1.6 CM
Tusk, gold; stereolithography
PHOTO BY ARTIST

Fabienne Vuilleumier
Untitled | 2007
3.5 X 2 X 1 CM
Medical plastic, quartz amethyst,
silver; thermoformed
PHOTO BY ARTIST

Charlene M. Modena
Endangered:
Gangotri Glacier | 2007
35 X 14 X 3 CM
Sterling silver, mica, diamond,
aquamarine, acrylic, polyester
resin; cast, bead blasted
PHOTO BY DONALD J. FELTON

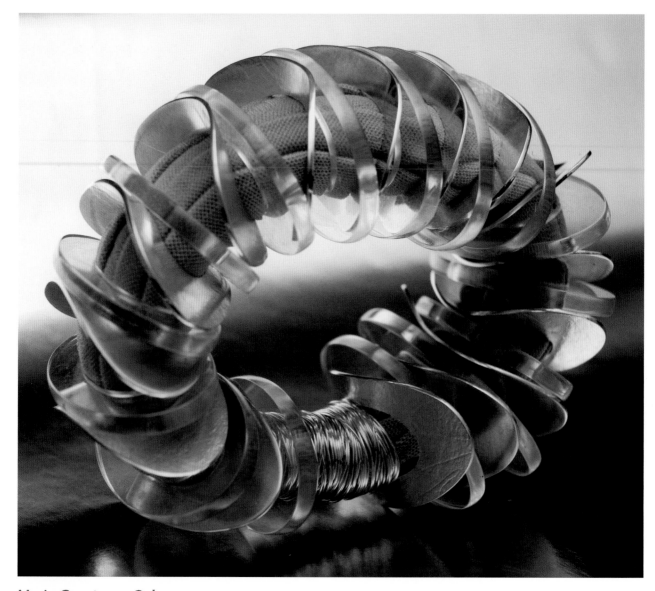

Maria Constanza Ochoa

Kiwi | 2005

7.5 X 9.5 X 4.2 CM

Plastic, sterling silver, textile;
sawed, bent, fabricated

PHOTO BY EMILIANO MOSCOSO

Vera Horsman

Chiseled Ring | 2005

2.8 X 3 X 1.5 CM

Sterling silver, acrylic; fabricated,
carved, riveted

PHOTO BY TREVOR JANSEN

Susanne Kaube
Überaschung | 2007
47 CM IN LENGTH
PVC
PHOTO BY ARTIST

Shana Astrachan
Gold Sequin Earrings | 2007
EACH, 10.2 X 4.5 CM
PVC sequins, sterling
silver; hand assembled
PHOTO BY CHRISTINE DHEIN

Ute Eitzenhöfer
Greetings from Idar-Oberstein 13 | 2007
7.5 X 6 X 2 CM
Smoky quartz, granite,
plastic; welded
PHOTO BY JULIAN KIRSCHLER

Krista McRae
Untitled | 2006
2.8 X 2.3 X 3.1 CM
Sterling silver, acrylic
PHOTO BY TERENCE BOGUE

Sadie Wang

Black and Grey Oval Pendant/Brooch with Oval Tubing | 2007

4.1 X 2.9 X 1.3 CM

Sterling silver, resin, onyx

PHOTO BY AZAD PHOTO INC.

Mary Hallam Pearse
Bling Brooch #2 | 2008
5.5 X 3 X 2 CM
Plastic, sterling silver, 14-karat gold,
diamonds; cast, fabricated
PHOTO BY ARTIST

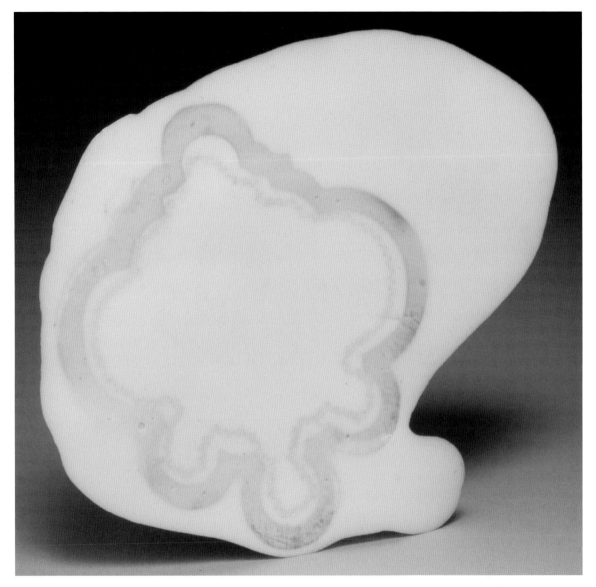

Kathleen Janvier

Residue Brooch | 2007

7.5 X 7.5 X 0.8 CM

Sterling silver, spring wire,
resin; fabricated, cast

PHOTO BY ARTIST

Sue Ann Dorman

Primitive Lizard God | 2004

25.5 X 14 X 2 CM

Black ABS plastic, metal;
fabricated, CAD/CAM

PHOTO BY ARTIST

Jan Matthesius
Carbon-Fiber Bracelet | 1985
12 X 1 CM
Carbon fiber, diamonds, resin;
fabricated in autoclave
PHOTO BY ROB GLASTRA

Kath Inglis
Cloud Brooch | 2008
5 X 8 X 2 CM
PVC, stainless steel; fabricated, hand colored, hand carved, skewered
PHOTO BY ARTIST

Eugenia Ingegno
Happy Widow | 2008
5 X 11 X 13 CM
PVC, silver; hand cut
PHOTO BY
MARGHERITA DE MARTINO NORANTE

Lin Stanionis
Untitled Brooch | 2008
10.2 X 10.2 X 1.9 CM
Urethane resin; cast
PHOTO BY JON BLUMB

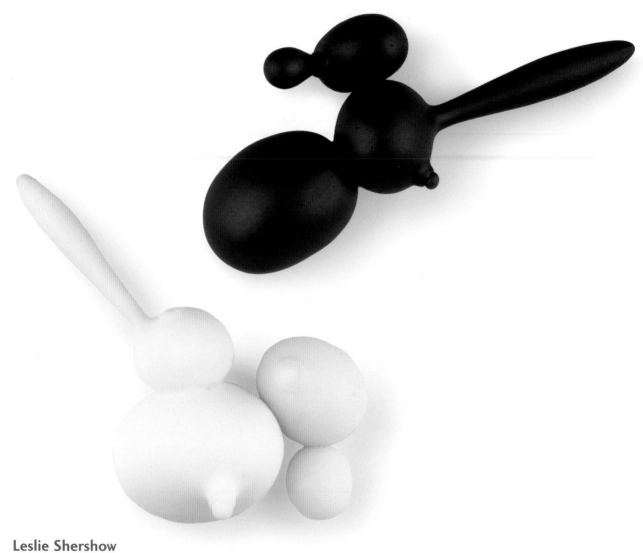

Leslie Shershow
Untitled (Brooches) | 2008
EACH, 9 X 5 X 4 CM
Epoxy resin, pigment,
magnets, graphite; cast
PHOTO BY KATIE MACDONALD

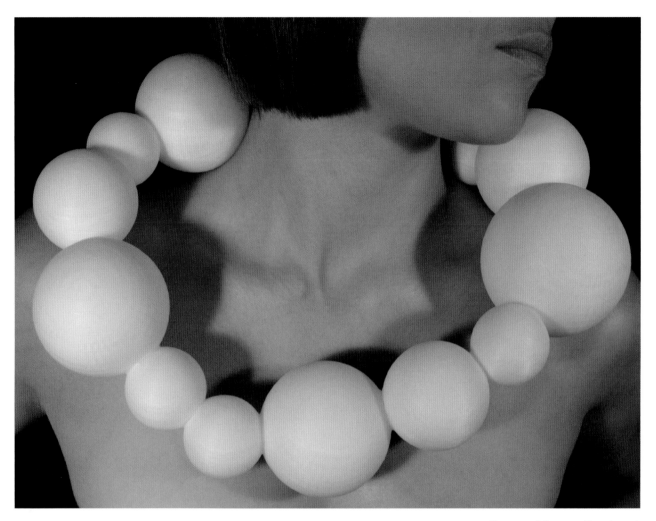

Donna Mason Sweigart
Sphere Necklace | 2006
15 X 30 X 23 CM
ABS plastic; fused-deposition modeled
PHOTO BY ARTIST

Silke Trekel

Necklace Message | 2007

27 X 24 X 0.5 CM

Onyx, calcite, laboradite;
reconstructed, cut, inlaid

PHOTO BY CHRISTOPH SANDIG

Anne Fiala
Big Lace | 2007
3.5 X 3.5 X 3 CM
Acrylic; laser cut

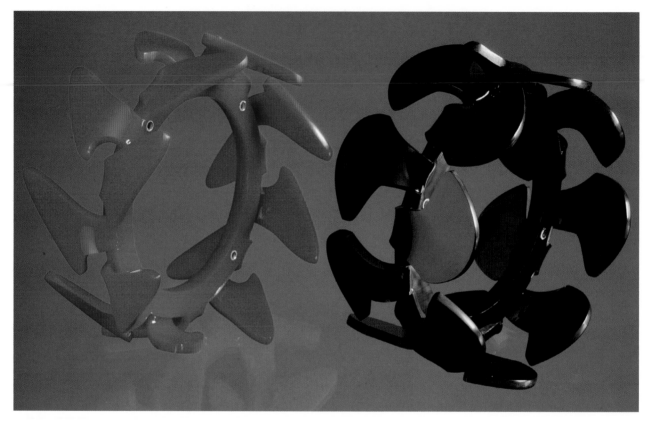

Laura Aragon
Untitled | 2003
EACH, 12.7 X 12.7 X 5 CM
Acrylic, silver; cut,
riveted, heat folded
PHOTO BY ADRIAN CAMPOS

Naomi Landig
Untitled | 2007
3.8 X 2.5 X 2.5 CM
Sterling silver, plastic
bottle, felt, spray paint
PHOTO BY ARTIST

Sujin Park

Folding II | 2007

34 X 16 X 2.8 CM

Plastic sheet, plastic
beads; scored, folded

PHOTO BY MYUNG UK HUH

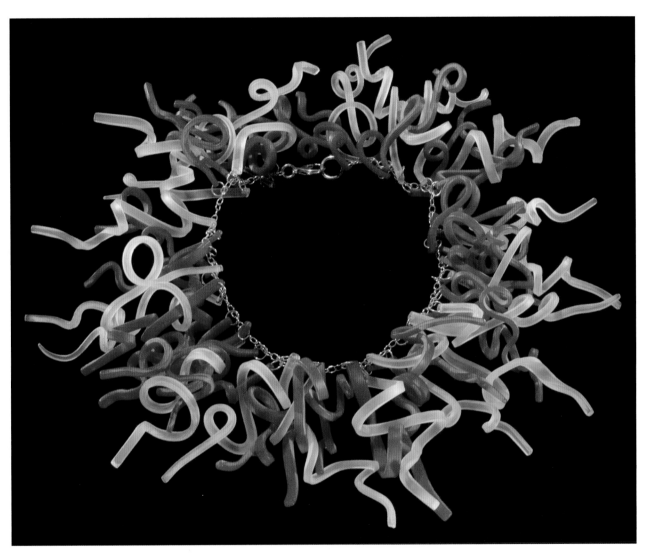

Edward Lane McCartney
Fire and Ice Neckpiece | 2006
6 X 32 X 32 CM
Acrylic sheet, sterling
silver; heat formed
PHOTO BY JACK B. ZILKER

Kenneth C. MacBain
Necklace | 2008
54 X 21 X 1 CM
Acrylic, sterling silver;
fabricated, riveted
PHOTO BY ARTIST

Sujin Lim

Blooming Bracelet | 2007

12.5 X 12.5 X 5.7 CM

Sterling silver, foam
sheet; fabricated

PHOTO BY ARTIST

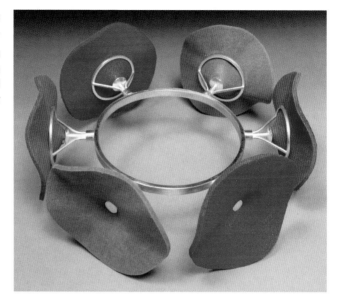

Carole Leonard

Spiral Ring | 2006

3 X 2.5 X 1 CM

Thermoplastic, silver;
filed, heat formed

PHOTO BY ARTIST

Carla Pennie McBride
Untitled | 2008

6 X 7 X 0.8 CM

Sterling silver, epoxy resin, mulberry
paper, India ink; fabricated,
stamped, inlaid, oxidized

PHOTO BY ARTIST

Inger Marie Berg
Red Happiness Necklace | 2002
23 CM IN DIAMETER
Translucent PVC sheet, silver;
hand fabricated
PHOTO BY TOR ALEX ERICHSEN

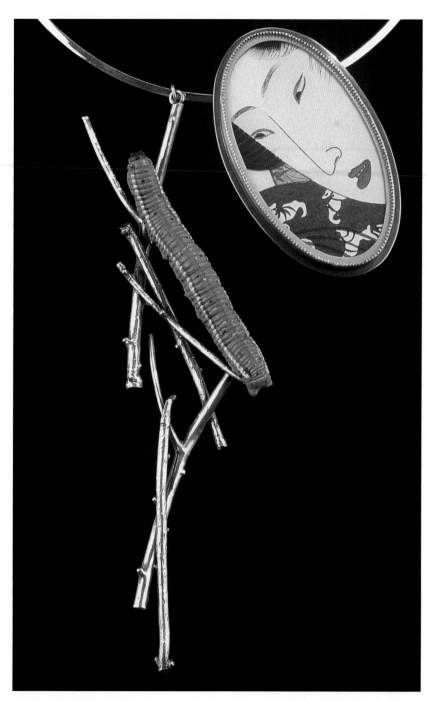

**Roberta Williamson
David Williamson**
Gentle Friend | 2007
CATERPILLAR DROP, 13 X 4 X 1.8 CM;
PORTRAIT BEZEL, 8 X 4 X 0.8 CM

Sterling silver, resin, plastic,
antique woodblock print, acrylic
paint; hand fabricated, bezel
set, lost wax cast, painted

PHOTO BY JERRY ANTHONY

Nicole Jacquard

Fragments 2 | 2008

2.5 X 5 X 6 CM

Plastic resin, fine silver, gypsum powder,
thermoplastic; rapid prototyped

PHOTO BY KEVIN MONTAGUE

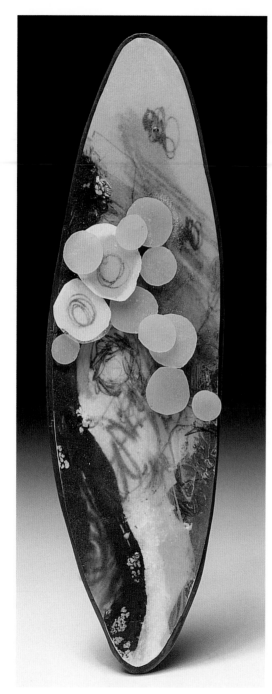

Susan Kasson Sloan
Resin Brooch I | 2005
14 X 4.4 CM
Epoxy resin, pigment,
sterling silver
PHOTO BY RALPH GABRINER

Natalya Pinchuk
Growth Series: Brooch | 2008
13 X 11 X 6.5 CM
Wool, copper, stainless steel, plastic fruit and flower
parts, sterling silver, waxed thread; fabricated, assembled

Andrea Wagner
Instrumentrics # 12 | 1998
4.5 X 7 X 4.5 CM
Sterling silver, epoxy resin,
pigment; rolled, sawed, bent,
soldered, multi-cast, sand
finished, polished
PHOTO BY ILSE SCHRAMA

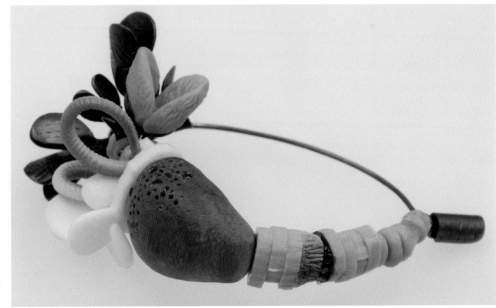

Karla Way
*Soothsayer's Cloakpin
(In Grey)* | 2007
3.5 X 9 X 6 CM
Thermoplastic, jarrah, plastic, copper, cubic zirconia,
paint; cold connected
PHOTO BY DOUGAL HASLEM

Fantasia Piper *refers to a vintage brand of Belgian pipe and to the type of bird called a piper. The head, beak, and foot of the piece were fabricated and retrofitted to a beautiful, old pipe. The orange color on the pipe is known as "butterscotching," a natural patina on Bakelite.* L & SC

Lisa Cylinder
Scott Cylinder
Fantasia Piper Brooch/Object | 2005
11.5 X 17.5 X 4.5 CM

Sterling silver, aluminum, brass, stainless steel, epoxy resin, vintage Bakelite pipe, gold leaf, paint, patina; fabricated, cast, carved

PHOTO BY ARTIST

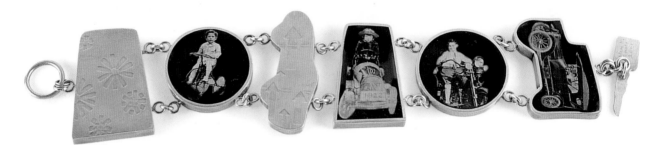

Ellen Kohn Gross

*Reversible Bracelet: Melinda Loves
Cars: Side I: Her Childhood* | 2001

4 X 20.5 X 0.5 CM

Sterling silver, photographs, pigment,
epoxy resin; fabricated

PHOTOS BY NICK GHIZ

Elise Kendrot
Spoonful | 2007
9 X 4.5 X 3.5 CM

Thermoplastic, found objects,
sterling silver, freshwater pearls,
bead cord; laminated, carved,
heat formed, hinged

PHOTO BY ARTIST

Hiroshi Kure
Driftwood Skull Ring | 2004
2 X 2.5 X 3.2 CM
Polyurethane, bronze
PHOTO BY TOSHIYA SUDA

Annie Tung
Gone? | 2007
PENDANT, 6 X 7 X 1 CM
Acrylic, hair, nylon; cast
PHOTO BY ARTIST

Erika Juzwiak

It Is Imperative That We Take a Closer Look at Ourselves | 2008

4 X 4 X 1.5 CM

Sterling silver, acrylic, found
objects; fabricated, riveted

PHOTO BY ARTIST

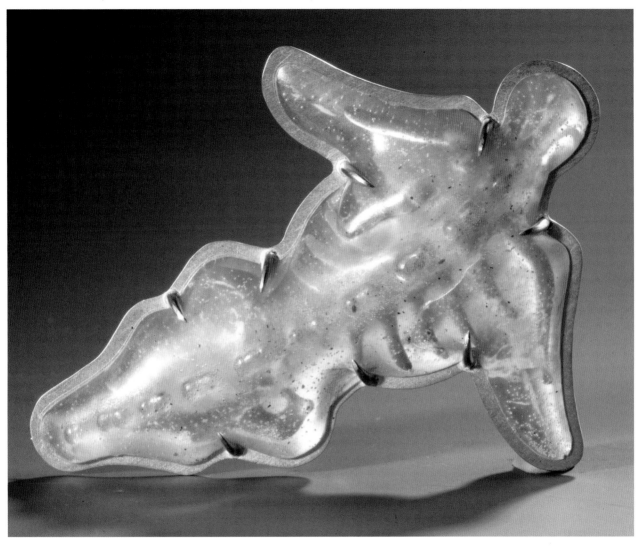

Lisa M. Wilson
Exoskeleton Ornament | 2008
6 X 9 X 1.5 CM
Nickel, resin, pigment;
cast, fabricated
PHOTO BY JEFF SABO

Alexis Pierre-Louis

Root Doctor (Ring) | 2008

6 CM IN LENGTH

Thermoset PVC, polyurethane,
steel wire, oil paint

PHOTO BY ARTIST

Mary Donald

Cocooning | 2008

7 X 2.5 X 3.5 CM

Latex, 18-karat gold, monofilament;
fabricated, burned, riveted

PHOTO BY PATRICK LIOTTA

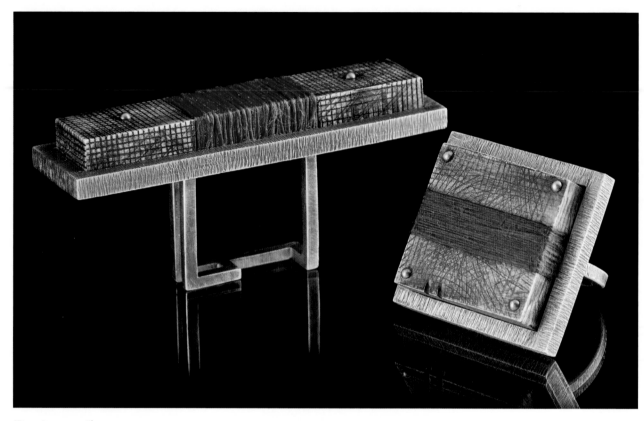

Zac Lopez-Ibanez

Your Presence Rings | 2008

LEFT, 2.7 X 6.1 X 1.6 CM

Sterling silver, brass, PVC, waxed linen thread, pigment;
fabricated, riveted, roller printed, textured

PHOTO BY MARY VOGEL

Emily Watson
Bubble Resonance | 2008
6.4 X 1.6 X 3.8 CM
Acrylic polymer, bowling ball plastic,
sterling silver; carved, fabricated
PHOTO BY ARTIST

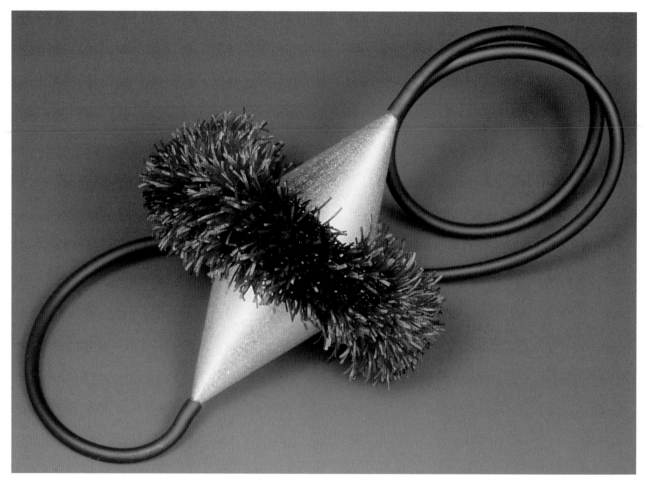

Jessica Davies

Double Cone Neckpiece | 2000

7.6 X 11.4 X 31 CM

Sterling silver, rubber, plastic;
raised, fabricated

PHOTO BY DON FELTON

Janet Lewis
Uncut Cable-Tie Necklace | 2008
44.5 X 44.5 X 10.2 CM
Plastic cable ties, plastic tubing,
metal wire; assembled
PHOTO BY GARY POLLMILLER

Yuka Saito

Kaichuka | 2008

15 X 12 X 4 CM

Sterling silver, polypropylene, moonstone

PHOTO BY ARTIST

Christine Dhein
Strictly Rubber Bog | 2007
120 X 12.5 X 12.5 CM
Recycled rubber bicycle inner
tubes, latex, recycled sterling silver,
plastic beads; fabricated, cast
PHOTO BY ARTIST

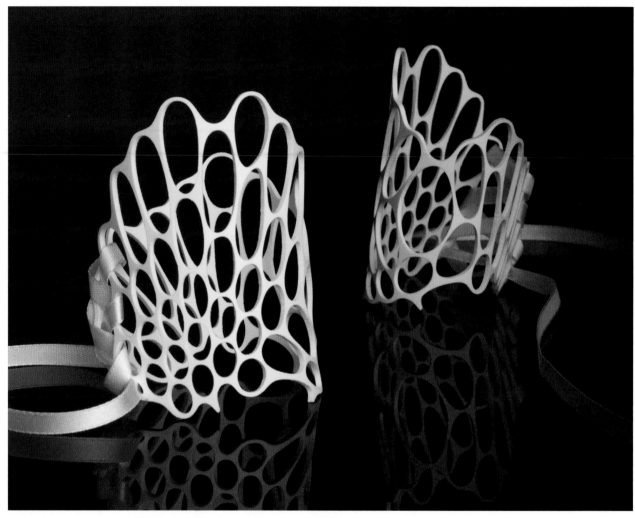

Nervous System
(Jessica Rosenkrantz and Jesse Louis-Rosenberg)
Radiolaria Bracelet | 2007
0.2 X 7.6 X 15.7 CM
Silicone rubber, silk; water jet cut
PHOTO BY SARAH ST. CLAIR RENARD

Andi Velgos
Specimen No. 0317 (Brooch)
Pectoricum I Auricula | 2008
15 X 10 X 7 CM
Copper, stainless steel, epoxy resin,
pigment; fabricated, formed
PHOTO BY STEFFEN ALLEN

Telma Simões

Bow (Brooch) | 2007

13 X 8 CM

Virgin rubber, silver;
pierced, fabricated

PHOTO BY TIAGO BRÁS

Nicole Jacquard

Fragments I | 2008

2.5 X 7 X 7.5 CM

Plastic resin, fine silver, gypsum powder,
thermoplastic; rapid prototyped

PHOTO BY KEVIN MONTAGUE

Katja Prins

Flowerpiece #1 | 2006

8 X 4.5 X 3 CM

Silver, plastic

PHOTO BY EDDO HARTMANN

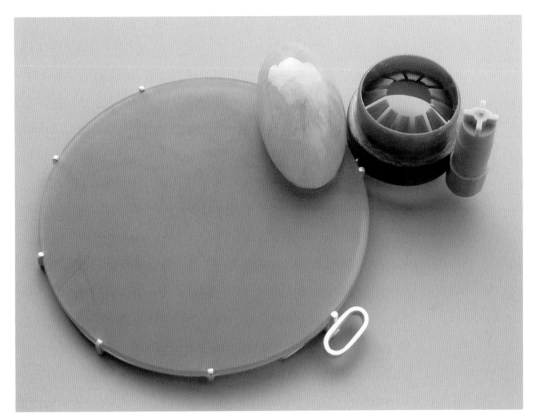

Jantje Fleischhut
Greens | 2007
7 X 2.5 CM
Silver, epoxy, found
plastics, quartz

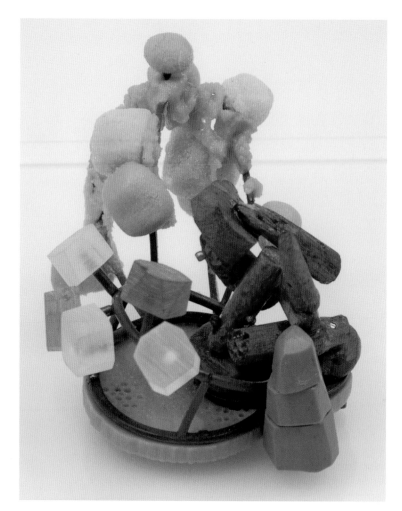

Karla Way

Metamorphic Rock (Brooch) | 2007

5.5 X 5.5 X 4.5 CM

Thermoplastic, sterling silver, copper,
brass, jarrah, sand, epoxy resin adhesive,
gold pigment; cold connected

PHOTO BY DOUGAL HASLEM

Amy Tavern
Honeyfelt | 2005
3 X 4.5 X 4.5 CM
Sterling silver, felt, resin; oxidized,
fabricated, dipped, sanded, riveted
PHOTO BY HANK DREW

Karen McCreary
Keyway Choker | 2005
11 X 3 X 0.5 CM
Acrylic sheet, lacquer,
22-karat gold leaf; carved
PHOTO BY HAP SAKWA

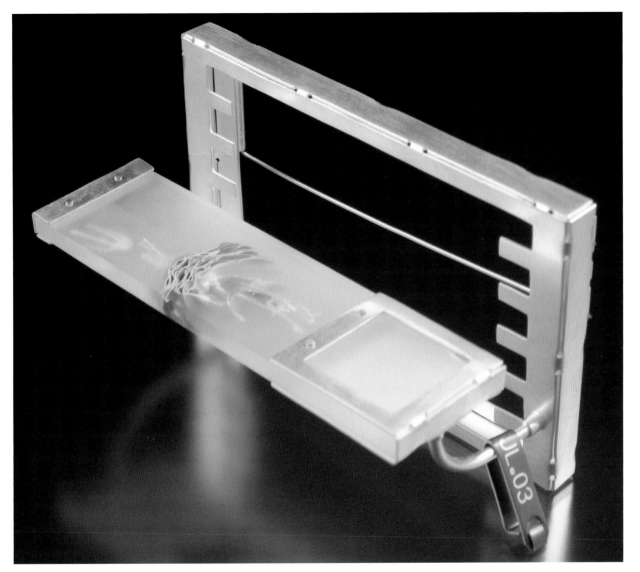

Nisa Blackmon

ZBSS.JL.03, Slide-Box Brooch with 036.5 Section | 2007

5 X 7.5 X 5.5 CM

Plastic flowers, plasticized paint, aluminum, sterling silver,
acrylic resin; dissected, recombined, tagged, dipped, embedded,
sectioned, fabricated, riveted

PHOTO BY ARTIST

Claudia Halder

Klunker Ring | 2004

4.1 X 2.2 X 1.8 CM

Plastic; heat formed, drilled, beaded

PHOTO BY ARTIST

Jiro Kamata

Sunny Pendant | 2005

7 X 7 X 1.5 CM

Silver, sunglasses; laser engraved

PHOTO BY ARTIST

Katja Kempe
Clunker Rings | 2005
EACH, 8 X 4.5 X 4.5 CM
Sterling silver,
acrylic resin; cast
PHOTO BY MALIN KUNDI

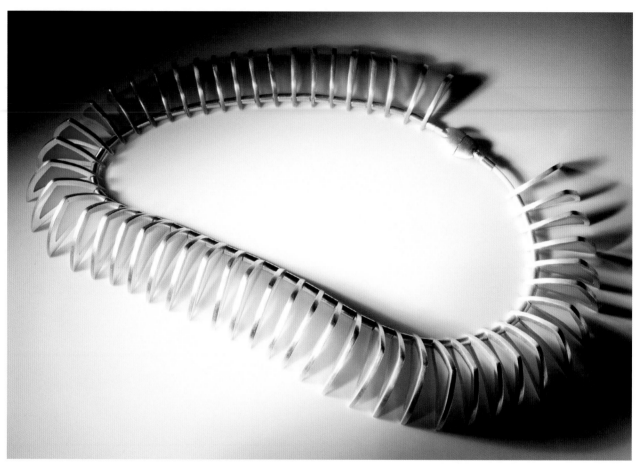

Cristina Betancur

Centipedes on Your Neck | 2007

1.5 X 20 X 20 CM

Sterling silver, resin, rubber;
cast, hand filled

PHOTO BY CAMILO ECHEVERRI

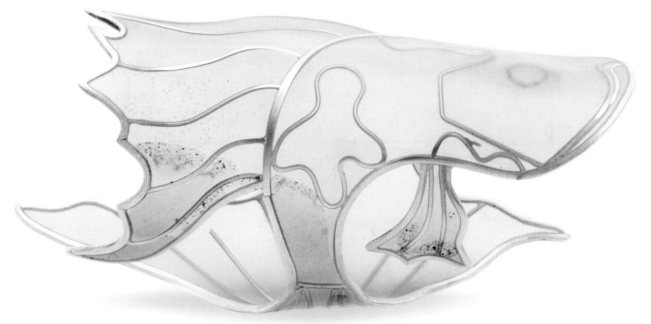

Lauren N. Pineda
Fish Cuff | 2007

14.5 X 12 CM

Sterling silver, polyurethane resin,
pastel chalk pigments; fabricated

PHOTO BY ANDREY CHEPUSOV

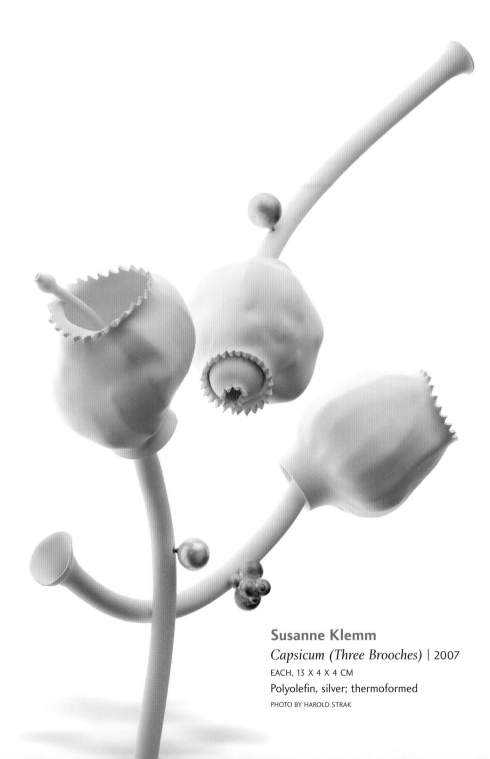

Susanne Klemm
Capsicum (Three Brooches) | 2007
EACH, 13 X 4 X 4 CM
Polyolefin, silver; thermoformed
PHOTO BY HAROLD STRAK

Rebecca Hannon
Camino Chain | 2005
30 X 21 X 0.2 CM
Rubber; hand cut
PHOTO BY ARTIST

Ki Dong Kwon

Flower Hair Sticks | 2008

LARGEST, 24 X 5 X 5 CM

Sterling silver, plastic cable
ties, onyx, mother-of-pearl;
fabricated, cast

PHOTO BY KWANG-CHOON PARK

Minna Karhu

Brooch | 2008

7.5 X 13.1 X 5.4 CM

Recycled plastic, silver,
steel; heat shaped, riveted

PHOTO BY ARTIST

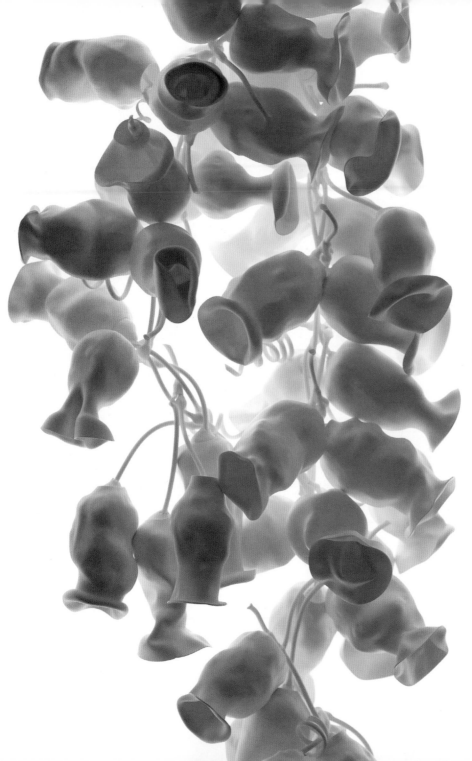

> I try to materialize my observations of nature by wrapping up a transitory object. When the object is unwrapped, only the thin plastic skin is left as a memento of nature. SK

Susanne Klemm
Boa (Necklace) | 2007
35 X 4 X 4 CM
Polyolefin; thermoformed
PHOTO BY HAROLD STRAK

Hiltje Wynia
Untitled | 2007
38 X 27 X 3 CM
Acrylic sheet;
formed, sprayed
PHOTO BY BIRGIT LAKEN

Ellen Himic
Bayonet Mechanism Brooch | 2005
13 X 13 X 4 CM
Epoxy resin; rapid prototyped
PHOTO BY SELECTIVE PHOTOGRAPHY

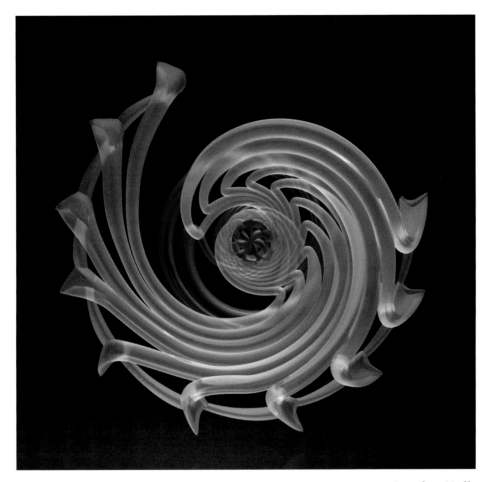

Jocelyn Kolb
Maelstrom | 2007
10 X 10 X 10 CM
Photosensitive resins, epoxy
resin; 3D modeled, printed
PHOTO BY ARTIST

Jocelyn Kolb
Punica | 2008
9 X 9 X 9 CM
Photosensitive resin, elastomer;
3D modeled, printed
PHOTO BY ARTIST

Karina Mihalus
Untitled (Necklace) | 2007
Thermoplastic; fabricated, laser
cut, thermoformed, sandblasted
PHOTO BY HARTMUT BECKER

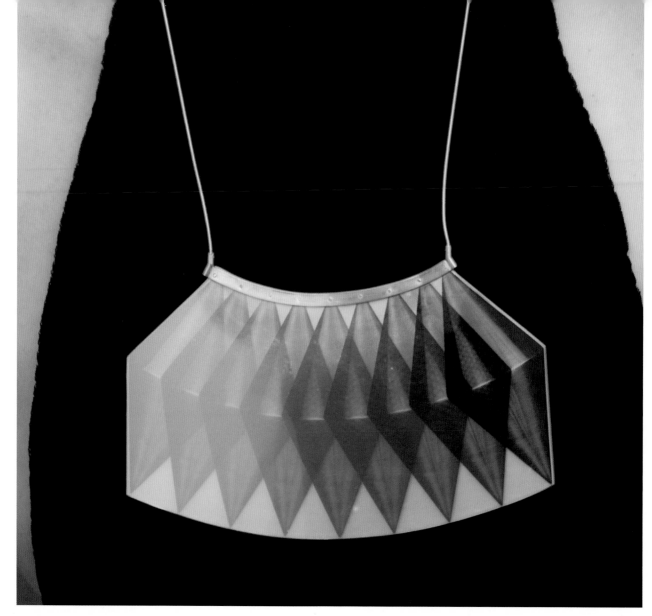

Anika Smulovitz

Body in Motion: Study 3 | 2007

13 X 20 X 0.5 CM

Sterling silver, 18-karat gold, transparency
film, silver cable; riveted

PHOTO BY TOM MCINVAILLE

Karin Seufert
Untitled | 2005
30 X 11.5 X 2.5 CM
PVC, thread; punched,
sewn, glued
PHOTO BY ARTIST

Leslie Shershow
Untitled (Pendant) | 2007
7.5 X 7.5 X 2.5 CM
Sterling silver, thermoplastic,
pyrite; fabricated
PHOTO BY JOHN SNEDEN

Uli

Pearl | 2004

52 X 20 X 0.5 CM

Silicone rubber, textile;
screen-printed

Iris Celeste Ledesma

Holding On Bracelet | 2007

20 X 2.2 X 1 CM

Brass, bronze wire, epoxy
resin; hand fabricated

PHOTO BY ARTIST

Joa Fraeulin
Manifestation II | 2004
45 X 24 X 12 CM
Wood, sterling silver, acetate
PHOTOS BY ARTIST

397

Christiane Schorm

Skies | 2008

1.2 X 4.5 X 61.5 CM

24-karat gold, photopolymers,
pigment; hand fabricated

PHOTO BY ELMAR WOLFF

Lea Marie Becker
Untitled | 2008
8 X 6 X 1 CM
Polystyrene, thread,
sterling silver, paint
PHOTO BY FEDERICO CAVICCHIOLI

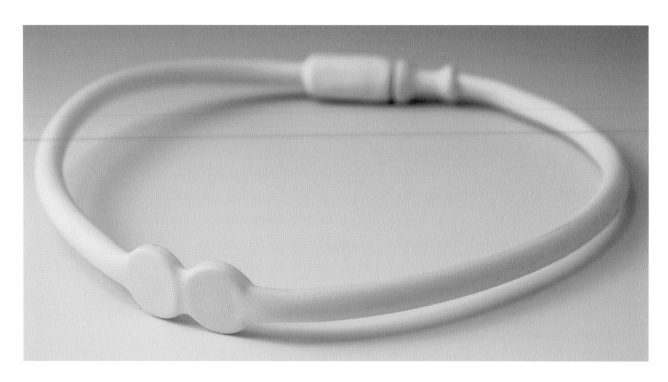

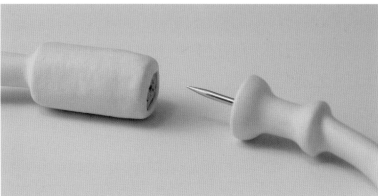

Soyeon Kim
Neckpiece I | 2008
35 X 0.6 X 1 CM
Plastic buttons, shrink
tubing, cork, pushpin
PHOTOS BY ARTIST

Sungho Cho
Recycling-Cutting | 2008
10 X 56 X 2 CM
Tire, sterling silver, pearls; cut
PHOTOS BY FEDERICO CAVICCHIOLI

Ela Cindoruk

Centerpiece Rings | 2005

EACH, 4 X 6.5 CM

Polystyrol, sterling silver, acrylic wall
paint; cut, fabricated, painted

PHOTO BY ARTIST

Mecky van den Brink
Collar of the Rim of a Plate | 2005
28 CM IN DIAMETER
Porcelain, chinaware, paper; laminated
PHOTO BY COEN DEKKERS

Karin Kato
QU4DRO | 2006
12.5 X 12.7 X 1.1 CM
Sand, resin, silver; cast
PHOTO BY ARTIST

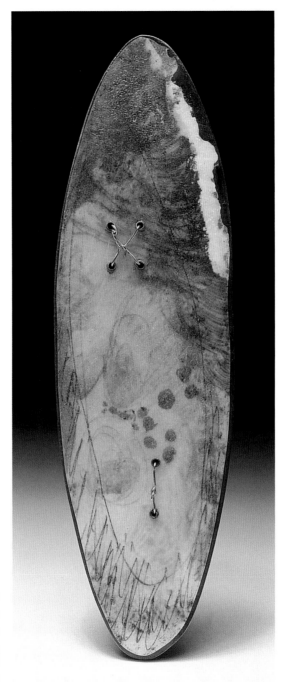

Susan Kasson Sloan
Resin Brooch II | 2005
15.2 X 4.4 CM
Epoxy resin, pigment, sterling
silver, 22-karat gold
PHOTO BY RALPH GABRINER

Vicki Mason

Violet, Blue, Brown Hybrid | 2008

5.6 X 11.2 X 1.7 CM

Copper, PVC, polyester thread; powder coated,
hand dyed, fabricated, cut, sewn, coiled

PHOTO BY TERENCE BOGUE

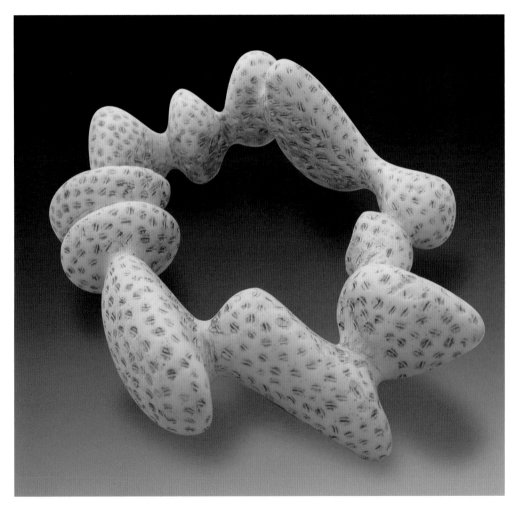

Moshiko Botser
Io (Bracelet) | 2007
5 X 12 X 16 CM
Polyoritan resin, pigment
PHOTO BY GILA KAPLAN

**Svetlana Rainous and
Youlia Rainous for alt&Go**

Abaca Deluxe Rings | 2006

EACH, 4 X 3 X 3 CM

Gum, resin, colored brass;
hand fabricated, riveted

PHOTO BY ARTISTS

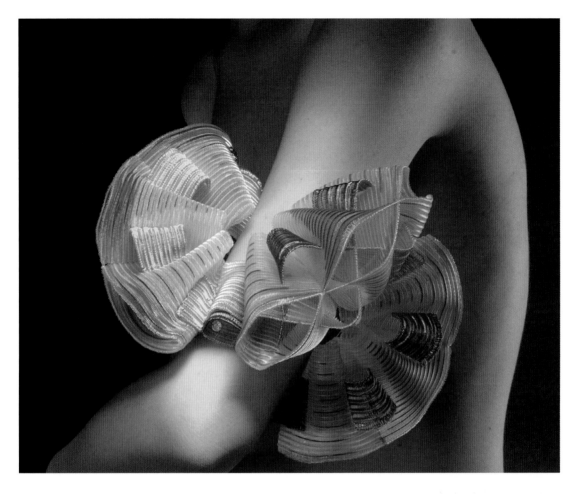

Anastasia Azure
Egg Hunt | 2007

20 X 20 X 20 CM

Nylon monofilament, color pigment,
wire; dimensional weave, inlaid

MAIN PHOTO BY HAP SAKWA
DETAIL PHOTO BY TOM MCINVAILLE

Cynthia Toops
Untitled Cuff Bracelet | 2006
10 X 10 X 4 CM
Industrial insulating tape, spring;
hand cut, hole punched
PHOTO BY ROGER SCHREIBER

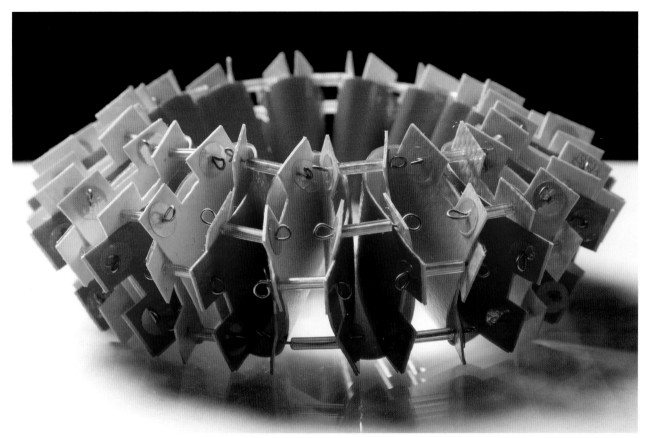

Jeanet Metselaar
Bracelet | 2007
3.5 X 11 X 3.5 CM
Plastic material
PHOTO BY BERT OTTEN

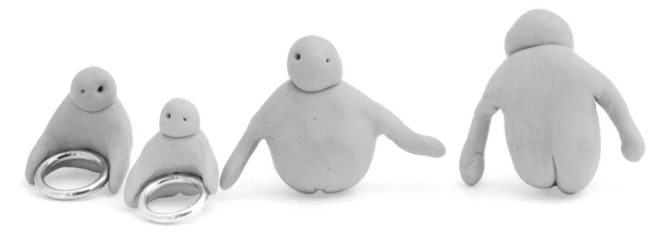

Margherita De Martino Norante

. . . *Che Fortuna!* | 2008

LARGEST, 6 X 5.5 X 3.5 CM

Vinyl polysiloxane, silver;
hand modeled

PHOTO BY JURI POZZI

Seainin Passi

Hot-Melt Glue Ring | 2007

10 X 5 X 5 CM

Embroidery thread,
ethylene-vinyl acetate

PHOTO BY RICHARD BOLL PHOTOGRAPHY

Felieke van der Leest

Lobster Necklace | 2000

22 X 14 X 6 CM

Plastic animal, stainless
steel, textile; crocheted

PHOTO BY ARTIST

Aud Charlotte Ho Sook Sinding
Parrot | 2006
25 X 8 X 10 CM
Silicone, silver; hollow cast
PHOTO BY ARTIST

Contributing Artists

A

Alexander, Melinda Long Beach, California 293

Allison, Fran Grey Lynn, Auckland, New Zealand 275

Andersson, Karin Roy Michelle Gothenburg, Sweden 204, 218

Aragon, Laura El Paso, Texas 340

Asbjørnsen, Marie Oslo, Norway 55

Astrachan, Shana San Francisco, California 327

Avellán, Ami Degerby, Finland 317

Ayudhya, Pirada Senivongse Na Bangkok, Thailand 16, 272

Azure, Anastasia Philo, California 76, 409

B

B., Stevie Dumont, New Jersey 244

Bachmann, Karen Brooklyn, New York 212

Baek, Jahyun Rita London, England 215, 282

Baran, Colleen Surrey, British Columbia, Canada 173, 302, 352

Barello, Julia M. Las Cruces, New Mexico 129

Bauer, Ela Amsterdam, Holland 117, 139, 160, 280

Bausman, David Laredo, Texas 241

Becker, Lea Marie Copenhagen, Denmark 399

Bekic, Lilyana San Diego, California 204

Berg, Inger Marie Norway 347

Berndt, Brigitte Regensburg, Germany 216

Betancur, Cristina New York, New York 380

Björke, Lisan Årsta, Sweden 32, 221

Björkman, Sofia Enskede, Sweden 243, 278

Blackmon, Nisa Bloomington, Illinois 124, 268, 377

Bodemer, Iris Pforzheim, Germany 279

Boekman, Ellie Vogeltown, Wellington, New Zealand 211

Borbouse, Camille North Bergen, New Jersey 296

Botser, Moshiko Kiryat Tivon, Israel 407

Bronger, Sigurd Oslo, Norway 240

Brossa, Maria Barcelona, Spain 9

Brubaker, Laura M.S. Nashville, Indiana 169

Burgess, Sarah Kate Philadelphia, Pennsylvania 102, 237

Büyükünal, Burcu Istanbul, Turkey 29, 53

C

Calderwood, Sofia Peninsula, Ohio 301

Carvalho, Ana Margarida Lisbon, Portugal 26

Chaney, Alexandra Ellensburg, Washington 249

Chang, Peter Glasgow, Scotland 104, 265

Chelminsky, Dania Tel Aviv, Israel 305

Chen, Tzu-Ju Warwick, Rhode Island 242

Chen, Yuh-Shyuan Kuantien, Tainan, Taiwan 82, 250

Choi, Aram Palisades Park, New Jersey 307

Choi, Sun-a Seoul, South Korea 144, 148

Choi, Sun Jin Seoul, South Korea 90

Cho, Sungho Florence, Italy 401

Christenson, LaVerne Fountain Valley, California 50

Chung, Hoyeon Carbondale, Illinois 92

Churchman, Joe Kalama, Washington 83

Cindoruk, Ela Istanbul, Turkey 402

Clausen, Jens A. Kautokeino, Norway 68

Cohen, Alexia Brighton, Massachusetts 158

Cohen, Barbara Vancouver, British Columbia, Canada 80, 300

Cowen, Caroline Gloucester, England 270

Crespo, Paula Lisbon, Portugal 74, 176

Cylinder, Lisa Oley, Pennsylvania 353

Cylinder, Scott Oley, Pennsylvania 353

D

Dancik, Robert Oxford, Connecticut 179

Davies, Jessica San Francisco, California 364

De Almeida, Estefânia R. Povoa De Varzim, Portugal 291

de la Porte, Alidra Alic Andre Copenhagen, Denmark 281

Deckers, Peter Upper Hutt, Wellington, New Zealand 163

Denning, Marianne Casmore Rødovre, Denmark 224

Dhein, Christine San Francisco, California 367

Dias, Cristina Stocholm, Sweden 113

Domash, Aimee A. Wildwood, Missouri 314

Donald, Mary Los Angeles, California 182, 193, 361

Dorman, Sue Ann Marina Del Rey, California 157, 332

Dunmire, Coco Florence, Italy 145, 223, 247

E

Edwards, Caroline Sydney, Australia 194

Eismann, Beate Halle, Germany 135

Eitzenhöfer, Ute Karlsruhe, Germany 328

Ellis, Stephanie Carbondale, Illinois 60

Engberg, Sara Hägersten, Sweden 127

Eo, Jin Sun Gyeonggi-do, Korea 75

Escobedo-Duran, Elva El Paso, Texas 81

Essor Biel, Switzerland 92, 294

F

Falkenhagen, Diane Galveston, Texas 232

Faris, Teresa Madison, Wisconsin 95, 286

Fechner, Lonny Copenhagen, Denmark 166

Fiala, Anne Indian Head Park, Illinois 339

Findeis, Karin Sydney, Australia 200

Fisher, Jaime Jo Austin, Texas 145, 266

Fitzpatrick, Shelby Ferris Surry, Kent, England 45, 245

Fleischhut, Jantje Amsterdam, Netherlands 13, 38, 62, 101, 174, 186, 187, 373

Fly, Karen Copenhagen, Denmark 206

Fok, Nora Hove, East Sussex, England 46, 123

Forsbrook, Gill Ely, Cambridgeshire, England 72, 299

Fraeulin, Joa Meilen, Switzerland 397

Frias, Javier Moreno Idar-Oberstein, Germany 255

Furuhashi, Motoko Saitama, Japan 69

About the Juror

Susan Kasson Sloan is a self-taught jeweler, studio artist, and educator. In the mid-1980s, she began working with epoxy resin, a medium that she loves for its wide range of creative possibilities. Susan continues to be intrigued with epoxy resin as a collage material that can mimic and morph whatever the imagination conceives.

Susan teaches regularly at the 92nd Street Y in New York City and The Art School in Demarest, New Jersey. Additionally, she has taught at Haystack on Deer Isle, Maine; Touchstone in Farmington, Pennsylvania; the Penland School of Crafts in Penland, North Carolina; the Maryland Institute College of Art in Baltimore, Maryland; the Pratt Institute in Brooklyn, New York; the Southwest Craft Center in San Antonio, Texas; and the Newark Museum in Newark, New Jersey.

Susan lives in Hillsdale, New Jersey. Her work is in the collections of the Renwick Gallery in Washington, D.C.; The Cooper-Hewitt National Design Museum in New York City; the Victoria and Albert Museum in London; and the Gregg Museum of Art and Design at North Carolina State University in Raleigh, North Carolina.

Acknowledgments

It was an honor to work with the wonderfully talented artist and juror Susan Sloan on this publication. We are in awe of her passion for, expertise in, and dedication to all things plastic. Susan's sincere appreciation for creative expression, technical ability, and raw talent turned our selection process into an exciting journey full of insight and discovery. Her thoughtful consideration of every single image has produced an outstanding collection that will impart value and inspiration to the contemporary jewelry field for many years to come.

I deeply appreciate the continued support of all the jewelers around the world who send images to be considered for this series. At their heart, these books are a celebration of their talent, creative vision, and dedication to their medium. I also wish to thank the galleries, schools, and organizations that promote contemporary jewelry, teach and inspire others, and advocate our publications.

Publishing is an amazing collaborative adventure. It takes a talented team of professionals to manage the multitude of details that comprise these books. Gavin Young was an incredible co-captain throughout this exciting experience. Paige Gilchrist, Kathy Sheldon, Julie Hale, and Dawn Dillingham provided indispensable editorial support. Chris Bryant, Shannon Yokeley, Jeff Hamilton, Bradley Norris, and Carol Morse supplied first-rate assistance in the art department, and Matt Shay gave us a truly gorgeous layout, design, and cover. Todd Kaderabek and Lance Wille kept us on track and on schedule. Thank you all for your talent, effort, and friendship.

—Marthe Le Van